A Medical Doctor Looks
at the Reality of Creation

# GOD
# MADE

A Medical Doctor Looks
at the Reality of Creation

# GOD MADE

## Isaac V. Manly, M.D.

 COLLEGE PRESS
PUBLISHING COMPANY
Joplin, Missouri

Copyright © 1994
College Press Publishing Company
Second Printing, 1995


All Scripture quotations are taken from the Authorized, King James
Version of the Bible.


Library of Congress Catalog Card Number: 93-74576
International Standard Book Number: 0-89900-676-0

# Table of Contents

# Acknowledgments

I wish to acknowledge my wife Peggy who has been a strong witness to me of God's love, and who has encouraged me to know and to enjoy God's Word. I am sure I would not have been called to write this manuscript without her witness and her patient support.

I am grateful to my four children, Kathie, Sawyer, Betsy, and Peggy for their interest in this material and for their encouragement.

My long-time secretary, Jeanne Poole, was most helpful in typing and my nurse, Pat Nelson, was kind to perform copying duties which are not included in her job description. More recently, Linda Dollar has also helped with the manuscript. Mr. David M. Hazard and Mr. Max Heine furnished technical advice and assistance in its final preparation.

I also thank Dr. Gerald Van Dyke, Chairman of the Triangle Association for Scientific Creationism, and Professor of Botany and Plant Pathology at North Carolina State University, Raleigh, North Carolina, for helpful suggestions.

I am thankful to God for the encouragement of my faith and knowledge of Scripture which I have received from Joe Thomas Knott, III, attorney and teaching leader of the Men's Class of Bible Study Fellowship in Raleigh, North Carolina, and from Reverend Everett L. (Terry) Fullam, Minister and Bible teacher extraordinaire.

George F. Howe, Ph. D. and the publications committee of Creation Research Society were most helpful to me in reviewing and making recommendations regarding the scientific material presented in *God Made*.

I am deeply grateful to John Hunter, editor of College Press Publishing Company, and his staff for sharing the vision I have had regarding the potential ministry of *God Made*. Mr. Hunter's mature advice and encouragement have meant a great deal to me and to this work.

Finally, everyone interested in creation owes a debt of gratitude to the Institute of Creation Research of El Cajon, California for their pioneering work in the science of creation, and in their continuing ministry of encouraging belief in God's Word as revealed in Genesis through research, publications, and seminars.

# Foreword

The unique way that Dr. Manly expresses his own personal odyssey through the maze of evolutionary thinking, that so pervades our society and especially our educational systems, will impress the reader of this book. I share with Dr. Manly a very similar journey, having been a theistic evolutionist (believing that God brought all of His creation into being through the mechanism of evolutionary processes), and then realizing that this position is totally untenable both from a scientific and a biblical position. The organization to which we both belong, Triangle Association for Scientific Creationism (TASC), is dedicated to educating Christians in the scientific evidences for Creation and how these evidences agree with the historical and spiritual teachings of Scripture.

Perhaps one of the key contentions in the whole creation-evolution debate pivots on the Noachian Flood. If one is a Christian (truly born-again by the Spirit of God) then one believes that Jesus is the Christ, the Son of God, the third person of the Godhead. Since Jesus refers to the Flood of Noah as recorded in Matthew chapter 24, it follows that it must have been an historic event. Because Jesus also affirms the first two chapters of

Genesis by referring to them in the tenth chapter of the Gospel of Mark, it also follows that these events are to be considered accurate. Additionally, God confirms the Genesis account in the Ten Commandments given to Moses as recorded in the twentieth chapter of Exodus. Therefore, we would expect that the evidences from earth history, and life on earth as we know it, would be consistent with the historical recordings of Scripture. In fact, that is what we find in Dr. Manly's book, an excellent resource to enable Christians to confirm their faith in the accuracy and trustworthiness of God's Word. It will also open minds to new understandings of the riches of Scripture in its application to our life and our place in the stewardship of the earth. In a time when we are being bombarded with extremist groups who would have us worship this earth and its creatures rather than the Creator, this work is a welcomed addition to the wealth of information that clearly establishes the rightful place of God's created beings in God's plan. I am confident that this book will touch many lives in a positive way and its message will be a continual resource for those who struggle with the question of origins.

C. Gerald Van Dyke, Ph. D.
Professor of Botany
North Carolina State University
Chairman, Triangle Association
for Scientific Creationism

# Introduction

Has the theory of evolution ever cast any doubt in your mind about the truth of the first two chapters of the book of Genesis? Several years ago a young engineer confided in me that his faith in God as Creator and his belief in the Scriptures as the inspired Word of God were compromised by the teachings of evolution. This was an intelligent young man who had been educated in public schools and at a good university. He had been raised in a Christian home and attended church regularly. The impact which the teachings of evolution were having on his spiritual life troubled me.

I became a Christian at an early age, having been blessed with Christian parents, and with the knowledge of Jesus Christ. When I was exposed to the teaching of evolution in premedical and medical education, I was able to accommodate evolution into the revelation of Genesis, and I had no serious problems with my faith. I had become what is recognized as a so-called "theistic evolutionist." I recognized God as the Creator of life itself, and I was content to accept the teachings of evolution, believing that God had used evolution to create the various forms of life which we recognize and enjoy.

I had accepted the "day" of Genesis as representing an era. The revelation of creation as recorded in Genesis was especially impressive to me because it was so "rational" and similar in sequence to the evidence of sequential development of the forms of life demonstrated in the geologic record. Many religions and cultures of the world, both sophisticated and aboriginal, have had a creation story in their lore. Most of these are quite confusing and irrational, and would make no sense to a person with a modern education. The creation account in Genesis is different. It describes God at work creating the heavens as well as the earth, and developing an environment into which He would finally bring man in His image for fellowship. It is an account of God carefully making provision for His children. The account is reasonable, logical, and loving. It is consistent with God's revelation of Himself as caring and as a loving provider and protector.

I was taught evolution in the premedical sciences and in medical school as an accepted theory or fact with evidences that seemed reasonable, logical, and incontrovertible. One of the most impressive "proofs" was claimed to be found in the embryological development of a fetus. This "proof" was described by the catchy phrase "ontogeny recapitulates phylogeny," and purported that as an embryo develops, it passes through the stages of evolutionary development through which its progenitors passed. The fish gills were especially noteworthy, and some modern textbooks still refer to some cysts in the neck as being of "gill slit" origin.

When I became aware of the conflict evolution created in the acceptance of Scripture by some Christians, I determined to study the scientific evidence of evolution and attempted to correlate this with the Genesis account. I determined to learn all I could about Darwin and his theory and about how God might have used evolution for His purposes.

What I have learned in the past ten years of review of recent scientific knowledge of cellular morphology and physiology, the code of life (*DNA*), and the lack of supporting evidence for evolution in the light of recent scientific evidence is a shocking rebuttal of the theory of evolution. For instance, I learned that the concept "ontogeny recapitulates phylogeny" was disproved at least thirty years before it was taught to me. The "gill slits" which have been described in human embryos are nothing but folds, and have no relationship to fish gills. Despite the fact that this concept has been thoroughly disproved and its author, Ernst Haeckel of Germany, was exposed as fraudulently misrepresenting drawings to popularize this theory, it is still being taught. The fossil record is claimed to prove evolution, but as discussed in a later chapter, this, too, is *not* true. New molecular evidence also disclaims evolutionary theory.

Because our educational institutions continue to teach evolution as an accepted theory or fact, it is imperative that Christians learn the facts so they can instruct their children at home and in the churches.

The concept of evolution can offer a dangerous alternative for those who resist the authority of God. Sir Julian Huxley, avid and imaginative evolutionist and atheist, who has urged "Evolutionary Humanism" as a substitute "religion," wrote in *Essays of a Humanist*: "Evolution . . . is the most powerful and the most comprehensive idea that has ever arisen on earth."[1] He also urged:

> Evolutionary man can no longer take refuge from his loneliness by creeping for shelter into the arms of a divinized father-figure who he himself created, nor escape from the responsibility of making decisions by sheltering under the umbrella of Divine Authority, nor absolve himself from the hard task of meeting his present problems and planning his future by relying on the will of an omniscient but unfortunately inscrutable Providence.[2]

This sort of substitutionary belief has influenced not only our educational system, but some of our theologians and church leaders as well. Men such as Sir Julian Huxley use pseudoscientific myth proposing the origin of life by chance and evolution to deny the glory and authority of God. The evolutionist has become more bold in his imaginings and in his claims while our theologians have grown more restrained.

In the following chapters Darwinian and other theories of evolution will be discussed with evidence to show a lack of scientific confirmation. Some facts about the complexities of the living cell with the wonders of its blueprint called DNA will be presented to demonstrate to the reader the impossibility of its origin by chance.

I believe the reader will agree with me it is fairy tale myth that "from so simple a beginning endless forms most beautiful and most wonderful have been and are being evolved," as claimed by Darwin.[3]

I am trained in the biological sciences and I have no training or special knowledge of geology. I do not intend to discuss the question of the age of the earth or universe. I understand the power of God to be such that He could have created the entire universe and all that it contains in the six twenty-four hour days. It is quite clear to me that time itself is an invention of God for earth and has no special significance in His kingdom which exists in eternity. I must leave debate about the age of the earth and the meaning of "day" to others. The theory of evolution absolutely requires the interpretation of an ancient earth, and evolutionary teaching has insisted earth's age to be over four billion years. However, there is convincing evidence that the geologic changes commonly taught by evolutionary uniformitarians to have required millions and billions of years are the result of more recent catastrophic events such as volcanism, earthquakes, glaciation, and the Genesis Flood.[4]

I believe the truth regarding the concept of evolution is untenable, whether the earth is four and one-half billion years old or several thousand. In the following chapters I will sometimes refer to time intervals as accepted by geologists where it is desired to emphasize that *kinds* have not changed.

This book is written to encourage the believer in his faith in Genesis as the revealed Word of God. I accept the fact that a non-believer cannot be brought to belief in God by intellectual argument. A non-believer has a real problem with the origin of matter in the universe as well as with the origin of life. The presence of matter and life is everywhere evident about him and if he cannot accept a Creator, he must seek other explanations. Evolution has served as an object of faith for many, and I am painfully aware that we can expect to continue to have our children subjected to its teachings.

I pray this book will be used by the Spirit to enlighten you to the truth of God's Word and strengthen you in your knowledge of Jesus Christ as the Lord, the giver of life. Amen.

[1]Sir Julian Huxley, *Essays of a Humanist* (New York and Evanston: Harper & Row, Publishers, 1964), p. 125.
[2]Ibid., p. 79.
[3]Charles Darwin, *The Origin of Species by Means of Natural Selection and The Descent of Man* (New York: Bennett A. Cerf / Donald S. Klopper, The Modern Library, 1936), p. 374.
[4]John C. Whitcomb and Henry M. Morris, *The Genesis Flood* (Phillipsburg, NJ: Presbyterian and Reformed Publishing Co., 1961); "Creation Research Quarterly," published quarterly by Creation Research Society, P. O. Box 28473, Kansas City, MO 64118.

# Choosing Between Two Opinions

Elijah did not mind overwhelming odds. The Old Testament prophet confronted Israel's King Ahab because he had forsaken God's commandments and followed after Baal. Elijah proposed a contest of power: In one corner, the idols, represented by 450 prophets of Baal and 400 prophets of the Asherah; in the other corner, Jehovah, represented by Elijah.

When everyone crowded around the prophets for the showdown on Mount Carmel, Elijah spoke to the real issue: "How long, halt ye between two opinions? if the Lord be God, follow him: but if Baal, then follow him" (1 Kings 18:21).

### Two Opinions

The same tension permeates today's conflict between belief in evolution and creation. Will we follow evolutionists' account of a world, even a whole universe, that created itself? Or will we follow God's account as revealed in Scripture?

These choices are, in a sense, "two opinions." Both require faith. Not only is it impossible to make an exhaustive proof of the biblical account of creation, it is impossible — in spite of evolutionists' pompous claims to hold the scientific high ground — to prove a creatorless account of the earth's origins, and the theory that man evolved from single-celled life. This book will show that Christians need not feel they have to synthesize the claims of evolution into their faith. *The sum of two opinions does not equal fact.*

God has given us something better than mere opinion or theory. He has given us a brief, yet comprehensive account of the earliest days of creation. As we explore the intricacies of life, we will see that *the first two chapters of Genesis reveal significant truths regarding creation and the foundations of our faith.*

### *Choosing Faith*

If you were to count the scientists who align themselves primarily with evolution, and the scientists who line up with the general account of biblical creation, you would find odds approaching that of the Mount Carmel massacre. As it turned out, though, it wasn't outnumbered Elijah whose blood was spilled.

He challenged the false prophets to see whose god would send down fire to consume a bullock lying on an altar of wood. The big team went first, calling on Baal, hopping around in ceremonial dance all morning. At noon, Elijah began to mock: "Cry aloud: for he is a god; either he is talking, or he is pursuing, or he is in a journey, or peradventure he sleepeth, and must be awakened" (1 Kings 18:27).

The enraged prophets resorted to gashing themselves with swords and lances. With their blood gushing all over the site, they called out to Baal until the evening. No luck.

Elijah repaired his altar, which the other side had destroyed. He ordered water poured over the wood three times. He prayed a simple prayer and God sent down fire, consuming the sacrifice and the water in a trench around the altar.

Elijah ordered the crowd to seize the false prophets. They were taken down to the brook Kishon and killed.

Two opinions clashed. One, due to faith in what is real, triumphed over the other, which was based on faith in a pagan cult. The source of truth in Elijah's day remains the source of truth today. How long will we linger between two accounts of man's origin on the earth?

After I became painfully aware of how evolution has sabotaged the confidence some Christians have in Scripture, I took it upon myself to see if evolution was true, if even a part of it was worth upholding. As a practicing surgeon, and as one who has followed Jesus since accepting Him as Lord when I was eleven years old, I was prepared to search deep into the mysteries of life and its creation. I did not want to hesitate between two opinions any longer. I wanted to be able to help those who were caught as I once was.

God was faithful to reward my investigations. But before I expose to you the suppositions of evolution, let's look at the simple, yet profound truth of creation God has shown us in the opening pages of the Bible.

## Science, History or Revelation?

When I operate to remove a portion of lung, I sometimes remove a portion of a rib. To do this, I split a fibrous covering of the rib, the periosteum, along the length of the rib and peel it back from the bony part. I cut the bone on each end, remove it, and pierce the back part of the periosteum to reach the chest cavity. Once I'm finished, I sew all the periosteum back together, only it's missing a chunk of rib inside. Then, in a miraculous evidence of God's design, the rib begins to regenerate within the periosteum. It takes months for the process in adults, but it works. A near-perfect rib can be reformed in a newborn in less than a month.

Has God bothered to speak to us about this arcane bit of medical trivia? I believe he has. Genesis 2:21-22 says God caused Adam to fall into a deep sleep and "he took one of his ribs, and closed up the flesh instead thereof; and the rib, which the Lord God had taken from man, made he a woman . . . ."

This is a small piece of revelation. It is by no means critical to salvation or our understanding of God. Yet it hints at a secret doctors would not discover until centuries later.

If God was giving a glimpse of physiology here, should we take Genesis 1-2 primarily as science? Or are these chapters *revelation* that touch on science, as well as other disciplines? Are they primarily a *historical* account, as is so much of the rest of Genesis? Or as some scholars argue, do they represent just another version of existing *myths*, like a Hollywood remake of an old movie?

God did not intend these two foundational chapters to be all those things. To see why, let's examine each area.

HISTORY: Most Bible scholars agree Moses wrote Genesis. But since all of the events in the book happened before his birth, chapters 1 and 2 are not regarded primarily for historical authenticity, though no historical facts there have been proven untrue.

Furthermore, the lack of documented historical information in Genesis 1-2 should not become a source of doubt for any Christian. Archaeological findings support the authenticity of other parts of Genesis and other Old Testament books, where there is more detail. Excavations and ancient inscriptions have confirmed the existence of cities, including Ur, Abraham's homeland; Nineveh, built by a descendent of Noah's son, Ham, and later witnessed to by Jonah; Hazor, Megiddo, and Gezer, three cities rebuilt by Solomon; Ezion-geber, where Solomon built a navy; as well as Laish, Ashtaroth, Pella, Ashkelon, Rehob, Beth-shan, Aphek, and Bethshemesh.

MYTHOLOGY: Mythologies of origins have been products of many cultures. A Pueblo myth traces man's ancestry to a spider with two little packages. In response to the spider's magical singing, a woman emerged. All Indians were said to have descended from this Spider Woman. A second woman emerged from the other package, and became the ancestor of all other races of man.[1]

Many other cultures have produced mythologies of origins. One of the best known is the *Enuma Elish*, the Babylonian creation story, dating to perhaps 3000 B.C. It has the god Marduk creating the earth and sky from the body of another god he defeated in battle.

The Egyptians, East Indians, Greeks — all produced creation myths. Other American Indian creation myths involve birds interacting with the sun or water. Like the singing spider, these tend toward the bizarre, and are frequently associated with violence or intrigue between gods.

The Genesis account, though it still requires faith, speaks of a loving God with infinite power creating a world that, as we will see, reflects overarching order and balance. There is no reason for the Christian to sever Genesis from the rest of Scripture, downgrading it to mythology.

SCIENCE: The lack of detail in Genesis 1-2, and the impossibility of repeating in a laboratory what took place, disqualify this passage as good science. It tells us what God made. But, when did He do it? How did He do it? All we know is that it was with His Word — apparently all He wanted to reveal on that count, which brings us to the only remaining choice.

REVELATION: God has many secrets not readily understood by man. Revelation, the process by which He gives us a peek into His mysteries, most closely describes the purpose of the Genesis creation account.

Through revelation, God orients us to eternal truths. Genesis 1-2 reveals, for example:

It was God who made the heavens, earth, plants, animals, and man.

He literally made them, as opposed to initiating a process by which they made themselves.

There is infinite creative power in God's spoken Word.

Plants, animals and man are to perpetuate themselves, and to do so *after their kind.*

Man is created in God's image.

God sanctified the Sabbath from the early days of creation.

Revelation also establishes relationships of things in God's kingdom. From Genesis 1-2 we learn:

In the beginning God . . . . (Gen. 1:1). He has ultimate authority.

Man is steward of God's creation.

Marriage is very sacred to God, who made woman from man's flesh. They become one flesh in marriage.

God's plan for family is revealed in Genesis 2:24. The man is to separate himself from other family ties and cleave to his wife.

God's desire is to bless man, and to have relationship with him.

### God on Center Stage

Were these really six ordinary days? I do not plan to add to the endless debate on this point because it is outside the scope of this book. But whether you take the creation days as literal or as eras, as in the common biblical phrase "day of the Lord" (Isa. 2:12, Joel 1:15, 2:1; Zeph. 1:7; Zech. 14:1, among others), you still must back up to a starting point. Most accounts of origins, biblical and otherwise, agree that there was a distinct point when things began.

The Bible's first statement gives the basics for the revelation of Genesis, a revelation clearly at odds with what evolutionists tell us: "In the beginning God created the heavens and the earth." God existed before the world existed. He was around before matter of any kind.

Furthermore, God was the Creator. He was not created by man, or fantasized by people looking to fill some innate need for a supernatural mover and shaker. As Creator, He knows what is necessary for the well-being of His creation.

Because He is Creator, He is the ultimate authority. He is king over the earth, king over the heavens. Man is subject to Him, as are the angels, including Satan and his fallen legions. Because He created everything in the earth, all morals spring from His decrees of right and wrong. Because those morals originate with eternal God, they are absolute — unchanging, rather than evolving, as applied evolution would have us believe.

God may grant limited authority to man, but God remains the ultimate judge, and expects man to judge according to God's system of justice. As a benevolent King, He established a covenant of blessing for His creation when man fulfills his side of the bargain — obedience. God thinks so much of His creation that He extends mercy upon mercy to cover the rebellion of His creation when man repents.

Genesis 1:3 introduces the creative power of God's Word: "And God said, 'Let there be light'; and there was light." Through the first chapter, God speaks into existence the rest of creation. This can be considered only as revelation; no scientific breakthrough will ever unravel the mystery by which the Word became light and matter. But as revelation, we know it as a precursor to the Word made flesh, the incarnate Word of God, the Messiah, whose destiny lay in the seeds of creation.

The same revelation is stated more fully in the opening

of the Gospel of John, where beginnings, light, Word and Christ are brought together:

> In the beginning was the Word, and the Word was with God, and the Word was God. The same was in the beginning with God. All things were made by him; and without him was not anything made that was made. In him was life; and the life was the light of men. And the light shineth in darkness; and the darkness comprehended it not (John 1:1-5).

Jesus was in the beginning with His Father. All things came into being through Him and for Him. The light that shines through His life illuminates the darkness of sin as well as the darkness of ignorance. Therefore, any philosophy of man's origins that does not acknowledge the lordship of Christ has automatically severed itself from the foundations of truth.

### First Things First

God, being who He is, could have chosen man to represent the handiwork of His first day's creation and sustained him with manna, but Genesis 1-2 reveals that God is, among other things, orderly. He created light on the first day. It was no arbitrary choice. Light has far-reaching significance, both in the physical and the spiritual.

The creation of vegetation came after light. Had vegetation preceded light, it would have died, starved of the light that fuels its photosynthesis. Though the creation of the sun, moon, and stars followed vegetation, the light created in verse 3, perhaps some kind of universal light of which we have no physical record, was sufficient to sustain plant life.

God's order is also reflected by His creation of vegetation in advance of the creation of animals. Plants are not directly dependent on animals, but animals must have plants to eat. Scientists recognize plants, therefore, as the first order of the food chain.

Furthermore, plants and animals have a symbiotic relationship that illustrates the larger scope of the Master's plan for creation.

A dandelion pushing its way up through the soil begins soaking up light energy to produce oxygen. Using carbon dioxide, through the reaction of chlorophyll, it also produces carbohydrates. Animals require those same two products — oxygen and carbohydrates. Animals complete the cycle by producing carbon dioxide, one of the gases plants require. Animals and plants, therefore, are mutually dependent.

## Chasing the Darkness

John's recounting of Christ and God's light — that the light shined in the darkness, and the darkness did not comprehend it — harkens back to the days of creation. On that first day of creation, God separated light from darkness. As revelation in the spiritual realm, we know that light and darkness speak of two distinct kingdoms. Jesus said: "I am the light of the world; he that followeth me shall not walk in darkness, but shall have the light of life" (John 8:12).

The light of life, manifest in Christ, is as necessary to our spiritual nourishment as sunlight is to plant life. Just as a flower will never blossom without the nurture of light, no person can reach their full potential ordained by the Creator without the redemptive light of Christ making alive that mysterious inner transformation.

The perfect order of creation was revealed succinctly in the pages of Genesis. As we will see, the marvels of creation are all about us. They testify to the mind-stretching plan of the divine being who ordained an orderly world. This evidence, like the revelation of Genesis, challenges us to choose between two opinions: Did life emerge through chance interactions of molecular mush? Or did a wise and loving God create it?

[1]Willis J. Gertsch, *The American Spiders*, 2nd ed. (New York, Cincinnati, Atlanta, Dallas, San Francisco: Van Nostrand Reinhold Co., 1979), p. 6.

# The Wonders of Earth

## Its Uniqueness Sustains Life

As I sit writing this chapter I am looking out to sea from the porch of our condominium. The wind is light today, and so the waves are gently rolling onto the smooth sandy beach. The blue water line at the horizon with the lighter blue sky is distinct. The warmth and light of the sun is a reminder that it is the sun which is the source of life-giving energy, comfort, and much of the beauty we enjoy.

High in the western sky there is a long vapor trail produced by a jet airliner. The jet is not visible, but I know from experience and the pattern of the vapor trail that this was produced by a machine. There is no machine made by chance, and no machine has created itself. Therefore, I surmise this beautiful plume in the sky is a cooperative effort of God and man. In our human pride, we are apt to jump to the conclusion that man invents and creates things and thinks up concepts. In reality, it is God who has created and man has been blessed to discover and make use of some of the many concepts of our Creator, always limited to the things He has created.

What is the significance of these messages emanating from God's creation? King David understood quite well, and God has not revised his programming since then: "The heavens declare the glory of God; and the firmament sheweth his handiwork" (Ps. 19:1).

What was apparent to David escapes so many today. Ironically, God's hand in this marvelous physical display is most invisible for many of those who have dedicated their lives to the sciences, especially those who have staked their understanding on a world that created itself. We can best understand the gap between Genesis and evolution with a brief survey of but a few of the ways God organized the earth to sustain life.

Until quite recently our appreciation of the beauty of earth has been confined to what we can experience on its surface and within its atmosphere. Astronauts have been able to see its beauty from space, and report it to be a very special and beautiful sphere. There is nothing like it in our solar system, and there is no evidence that there is anything like it in the universe. Those who have seen earth from space claim its blue sky and cloud masses make it an object of incredible beauty.[1]

One does not have to leave earth to appreciate the beauty of its surface or its atmosphere. The sky furnishes a panorama of color. The sunset can be expected to produce a beautiful display any time it is not hidden by clouds. Clouds themselves add variety to the beauty of the blue sky.

## Environmental Tightrope

Earth is the only known planet with an atmosphere capable of sustaining life as we know it, or as we can even imagine it. The ocean of atmosphere is much larger than the ocean of water. The immense number of atoms and molecules in this ocean is absolutely necessary to protect life from destructive forces of many kinds. Meteoroids enter our atmosphere in enormous numbers, but most are destroyed by burning produced by the heat of friction of air. Primary cosmic-ray particles bombard our atmosphere from outer space in huge numbers, and if they reached the surface of our planet, they would be lethal to all life. These particles are broken up by collisions with atoms and molecules in the atmosphere, and become so-called secondary particles. These secondary cosmic-ray particles are harmless.

Of extreme importance, and of great recent interest, is the protection provided life by the ozone shield. Ozone, or "heavy oxygen," contains three atoms of oxygen in each molecule, whereas ordinary oxygen ($O_2$) which is necessary for respiration contains two atoms. The ozone shield is located about fifteen miles above the surface of earth and absorbs much of the ultraviolet radiation coming from the sun. Like cosmic rays, these ultraviolet rays would be capable of destroying all life if not reduced significantly by this ozone shield. It is also quite apparent there could have been no spontaneous origin of life by chance before there was an effective ozone shield. Yet the ozone shield is dependent on there being a plenteous supply of oxygen provided by living plants, which would have been impossible without an effective barrier to ultraviolet rays provided by the ozone shield. This fact has provided those who deny a Creator an absolute dilemma for which there has been no reasonable answer.

The visible rays from the sun are able to pass through the ozone shield without hindrance to warm the surface of earth. This has to be accepted as an incredibly convenient situation (one which may be considered a miracle) when compared to the problem encountered by lethal cosmic and ultraviolet rays. The heat rays are reflected in infrared wave lengths, and are absorbed by carbon dioxide and water vapor in the atmosphere. Thus, most of the heat from the sun is retained. Because the heat absorbed in the atmosphere of different areas of earth is not uniform, convection currents are created. These currents are influenced by the rotation of earth, producing winds. These winds help to distribute the heat from equatorial regions and those areas receiving more direct sunlight to the colder areas of earth.

The atmosphere is composed of a mixture of air, water vapor, smoke and dust particles, all of which are necessary for its effective function. The air is a mixture of oxygen (21%), nitrogen (78%), carbon dioxide (0.03%), and traces of other gases such as helium. As everyone knows, the oxygen is necessary to sustain animal life. However, it is important to understand the percentage of oxygen contained in air is exactly correct to provide the environment for life. A lower percentage would not allow combustion, and a higher percentage would provide an explosive environment in which every lightning discharge and every spark could produce a catastrophe.

Carbon dioxide is necessary for plant metabolism whereby carbohydrate is produced as an energy source through the enzymatic activity of chlorophyll utilizing the energy of sunlight. Oxygen is a miraculous byproduct. As with oxygen, the percentage of carbon dioxide in the air is of extreme importance to the function of the atmosphere in providing an acceptable environment. Too much carbon dioxide would result in the absorption of excessive infrared radiant heat and the consequent rise in world heat with disastrous results.

## *One Big Vivarium*

The oxygen-carbon dioxide balance of earth is apparently maintained by extremely sensitive balances perpetrated by the environment itself. Oxygen is supplied primarily by the metabolic processes of plant life. Carbon dioxide is a by-product of all sorts of combustion, including the burning of fossil fuels and wood and the metabolism of animals. A vivarium is readily constructed as a closed system which includes a proper balance of plant and animal life, and the atmosphere generated will support the enclosed living things for indefinite periods. The world is actually a very large vivarium. Of major concern at this time is the world environmental impact produced by the destruction of large areas of plant life, and the simultaneous increase in the burning of fuels of various sorts. An increased carbon dioxide level of the atmosphere could significantly affect world temperature levels with effects which are not completely predictable. It has been estimated that the vegetation of earth at this time produces 400 billion tons of oxygen by combining 150 billion tons of carbon with 25 billion tons of hydrogen.[2] Is this not a cleverly designed system which not only supplies, but regulates precisely the levels of these two elements which are essential for the metabolism of both plants and animals? The supply of each is not only interdependent, but inexhaustible if not interfered with by man's pollution. In Genesis 1 and 2 God ordained man to be His steward, to have dominion over all animal life and to tend to vegetation.[3] As we learn more about these intricate relationships of our environment, we realize that our lives in the flesh are as dependent as our spiritual lives on our obedience to His will.

### Water Everywhere

After describing the character and components of earth's atmosphere as being absolutely essential and miraculous, it is perhaps surprising to claim that water is even more essential, unique and miraculous. Nevertheless, water does indeed fulfill such a claim. All of life as we know it or can even imagine it, is completely dependent on water and the metabolic processes of life are related to the characteristics of water.

Water is the most universal of all solvents, meaning it

can dissolve more substances than any other liquid. Solid substances have a difficult time reacting with each other, but when dissolved in water their elements are freed to interact. Thus, chemical reactions and metabolic processes are encouraged. Our bodies are 70% water, and we require one and one-half quarts per day. Humans can go eighty days without food, but only ten days without water.

The water molecule is composed of two atoms of hydrogen and one atom of oxygen ($H_2O$). Is it not passing strange that water, composed of hydrogen and oxygen, occurs in significant amounts on no other planet in our solar system? Some scientists claim there may be other planets in the vast universe which contain such large quantities of water, but there is no proof. It is clearly the most significant substance on earth which supports life, and gives earth its unique characteristics. The surface of the moon, which lacks water, stands in sharp contrast to the surface of earth. It is not only lifeless and dull gray in color, but it exhibits persistent scarring of past injuries produced by falling meteorites. The action of water smooths earth's surfaces and life provides color and beauty.

Scientific theories are very tenuous and uncertain regarding the possible origin of water on planet earth. Comparing other planets in our solar system with the earth yields no convincing clues as to why earth alone possesses plenteous water. Miracles are heaped upon miracles.

Reverend Everett L. Fullam[4] has given witness to the

renewing power of water. He has related that he was once flying over an Iranian desert in a jet plane when he saw in the distance a dark square in the light sandy plain. As the plane drew nearer he saw that this was in reality a lush green oasis, but being perfectly square he realized it was designed by human ingenuity. On inquiring from the stewardess, he learned that while drilling for oil, a copious artesian well of water was tapped. As an experiment, this water was used to irrigate one square mile of desert with no planting of extraneous new seeds. The result was the lush growth he observed. He likened this to the working of the Spirit upon seed already planted by the witnesses of God's people. God has taken pains to demonstrate His power in the things He has created so we may understand the invisible blessings of His Godhead.[5]

In the normal temperature ranges of the vast majority of the surface of earth, water is the only substance which occurs naturally in three physical states — solid, liquid, and gas. Like other liquids, water becomes heavier as it cools and so cool water sinks. However, as it becomes cold enough to turn into solid ice, it floats to the surface. No other substance except bismuth behaves in this manner. If ice behaved like all other solids, it would sink to the bottom and fill deep lakes and polar oceans. Being insulated from direct sunlight, very little thawing would ever occur, and liquid water would become scarce. Life would become tenuous at best. Rather than sink, ice floats on the surface and insulates the underlying liquid water. The organisms living beneath the surface live on, awaiting the thawing which comes with the spring sunshine.

Ocean water contains many dissolved substances, of which sodium chloride (ordinary table salt) makes up about 78%. Seventy-one percent of the earth's surface is covered by oceans averaging two and one-half miles deep. The Pacific Ocean covers one-half of the surface of earth. Streams and lakes contain less than one percent of earth's water. Underground water equals about ten percent of the total in the oceans. This underground water is available to the roots of plants by capillary action and is essentially the primary source of water for land plants.

## Nature's Heatpump

Water has the highest *"specific heat"* of all compound substances. Specific heat is that amount of heat necessary to raise the temperature of a unit weight of any substance one degree centigrade. Most other substances have specific heats of less than one-half that of water.[6] Thus, water is capable of storing large quantities of heat with relatively little temperature change. The vast amounts of heat delivered to tropical waters by the sun is stored and transported to distant cold areas. Because of its high specific heat, the tropical waters seldom rise above 85° F. This warm water circulates and dispenses heat to the colder areas of earth. Many areas of earth would be quite uninhabitable without this heat distribution.

A person can experience the benefits of water's high specific heat when walking on a beach during a summer mid-day. The sand becomes extremely hot to our feet, but the ocean water breaking on the beach is cool and refreshing. The same number of heat rays strike the water and the sand, but the water remains near 80°, while the sand becomes uncomfortably hot. This miraculous physical quality of water not only cools our feet, but moderates the climate of our entire planet.

The Gulf Stream is a classic example of this mechanism of climate moderation. At its origin it is about fifty miles wide, flows five miles per hour, and carries about one hundred cubic miles of sea water per hour. Each cubic mile of this heated water is capable of delivering 184 trillion BTU of heat to the British Isles, or the heat equivalent to burning 7 million tons of coal. Heated air, flowing as trade winds, produces most of the power for this enormous flow of water by pushing the heated water into the Gulf of Mexico, out of which it flows.

Another heat exchange system works by the evaporation of heated water. Much energy is absorbed as liquid water is changed to water vapor, and is released as the vapor is deposited as rain or snow. Thus, through the combined circulation of water and air utilizing the three forms of water with its specific heat, there is remarkable moderation of earth's climate. Without this heat exchange system much of the earth would be uninhabitable or very unpleasant.

The earth is appropriately enough exactly the right distance from the sun (93 million miles) to provide the correct amount of light and heat. If it were significantly closer to the sun, its water would boil away, and if it were farther from the sun it would be a frozen planet. Its twenty-four hour rotation is also extremely important. If its rotation were significantly slower, extreme temperature fluctuations would result in most parts of earth.

### The Perfect Angle

Another quite miraculous gift to life is the twenty-three and one-half degree angle of tilt which earth's axis possesses. This produces our seasons. As the earth travels around the sun each of the poles points toward the sun in summer and away from the sun in winter. It is the angle at which the sun's rays strike earth, rather than distance alone, which determines the amount of heat delivered. Light delivers twice as much heat to a surface at a right angle than at an angle of thirty degrees. Summer comes to an area of earth when the rays are more nearly at a right angle. There would be no change of seasons without the twenty-three and one half degree tilt. However, if the tilt were greater the seasons would be extreme, with unbearable heat in summer in the major areas of earth and bitter cold in winter. Life would not be impossible, but it would be less enjoyable. The tilt of twenty-three and one half degree is a true blessing which we cannot appreciate nor be properly thankful for until we realize this gift. Those who refuse to honor God as Creator are given up by Him to their own deceits, as warned by Paul in Romans 1. We who acknowledge Him do well to learn of these wonderful blessings, and to teach them as His gifts to our children.

## *Miracle of Carbon*

The element carbon is one of the most important elements in the molecular structure of living things. This being so, one might think carbon to be a most ordinary element. However, the presence of carbon on earth is a true miracle, and carbon is much less abundant than hydrogen, helium, and oxygen. Dr. Owen Gingerich of the Harvard Smithsonian Center for Astrophysics has pointed out that a carbon atom can be made by merging three helium nuclei.

> This merging would be impossible except for the fact that there is precisely the right resonance within the carbon atom that encourages the process. Here, a relationship is found between oxygen and carbon atoms. Oxygen can be formed by combining three helium and carbon nuclei, but the resonance level in the oxygen nucleus is just one half of one percent, too low for the combination to stay together in significant amounts. If the resonance level in the carbon were four percent higher, there would be practically no carbon. If the resonance level in the oxygen nucleus were only one-half of a percent higher, virtually all of the carbon would have converted to oxygen. Because life is dependent on carbon there would be no life without this miraculous nuclear arrangement.[7]

Of the "scientific" theory of origin, Robert Jastrow,

Professor of Earth Sciences at Dartmouth University, has said,

> At this moment it seems as though science will never be able to raise the curtain on the mystery of creation. For the scientist who has lived by his faith in the power of reason, the story ends like a bad dream. He has scaled the mountain of ignorance; he is about to conquer the highest peak; as he pulls himself over the final rock, he is greeted by a band of theologians who have been sitting there for centuries.[8]

[1]Allen L. Hammond, "The Uniqueness of the Earth's Climate," *Science*, Jan. 24, 1975, 245.

[2]Thomson King, *Water: Miracle of Nature* (New York: The MacMillan Co., 1963), p. 22.

[3]Genesis 1:28 and Genesis 2:15.

[4]Reverend Everett L. Fullam, personal communication, 1983.

[5]Romans 5:20.

[6]Thomson King, p. 22.

[7]Owen Gingerich, McNair Lecture, University of North Carolina, Chapel Hill, NC, Feb. 22, 1983.

[8]Robert Jastrow, *God and the Astronomers* (New York: W. W. Norton and Co., 1978), p. 116.

# Charles Darwin: A Man for His Time

Charles was considered an ordinary boy. His teachers, in fact, considered him to be unmotivated, below average in intelligence. Little did they expect that Charles would grow up to change the world in ways they never would have imagined.

Born in 1809, Charles Robert Darwin was the grandson of Erasmus Darwin, a noted physician and naturalist. In the 1790s, the elder Darwin had proposed a theory of evolution which he described in a book entitled *Zoonomia*. According to Charles Darwin's biographer, psychologist John Bowlby, Darwin was well acquainted with this publication, and his own theories appear to be considerably influenced by those of Erasmus.[1]

If Charles Darwin truly lacked motivation, he somehow overcame it in his early adult years. Collecting plant and animal species far away from his native Shrewsbury, England, and pondering their diversity, he wrote books about his theories of why species differ. Darwin may have been a dull student, but his works eventually turned the rudder of modern thought. Largely because of him, natural science has charted new courses for the last 130 years. Darwin has done more than any one man to undermine the faith of many in the Genesis truth that God made the world we see.

### Toward Perfection

Darwin's life was preceded by the Renaissance and the Age of Enlightenment. After centuries of teaching by the Catholic Church that emphasized man's sinfulness and the need for ritualistic forgiveness and cleansing, a new era had dawned.

Artists and writers began to look at what they considered to be the bright side of man. Perhaps brightest of all was the potential for change. If man was innately good, as the early humanists believed, he could progressively get better and better, both as an individual and as a society. Many came to see man's destiny as resting in his own hands, not in God's. Rationalism, coupled with skepticism about established dogmas, marked the eighteenth century's Enlightenment.

These religious/philosophic trends eventually impacted politics. About three decades before Charles Darwin's birth, something else of historical significance was born — the United States of America. Darwin's homeland had been humiliated. It was not just losing a war, though that was costly and painful enough. Something new was in the political air.

The colonists were ripping off the shackles of monarchy, a system that had served noble Europe so well for centuries. They had formed a democratic republic, a system of self-government predicated on equal representation. There was no place for kings and queens and royal palaces.

Of course, no one knew if it would work. But in the flurry of political excitement, the seeds of change, like a contagious disease, took root in France. Before the 18th century was over, there was great turmoil and bloodshed, as the French Revolution sought to imitate what had transpired overseas. The landed gentry of France no longer had the authority they had enjoyed for so long.

To the western intelligentsia, it began to appear that the government itself was evolving — from the outdated monarchy to self-government. This transition boded great things for the dignity and prosperity of mankind.

England may have missed the boat regarding the onset of democracy, but it remained a political and intellectual contender. Her empire was at its zenith. From the tiny British Isles were ruled colonies around the globe, seeding what the English considered to be the most highly evolved civilization to date. At home, reform institutions such as the Salvation Army and orphanages were attacking poverty and other social ills. Industrialization, though not without its ills, was delivering tremendous productivity and producing for the first time a real middle class.

Some of the more optimistic observers felt they were moving toward the perfect society. The idea of Utopia, first spelled out by Sir Thomas More in a book of that name published in 1516, became a buzzword. As Darwin's writings began to shake society, other Utopias were put forth in Samuel Butler's *Erehwon* ("nowhere" spelled backwards) (1872); Edward Bellamy's *Looking Backward* (1888); and H. G. Wells's *A Modern Utopia* (1905).

Western culture in the nineteenth century was ready to soak up the intellectual showers that came forth from Darwin and his contemporaries. His theories, postulating an inexorable force driving every creature toward higher and higher levels of perfection, fit tongue-in-groove with a culture that believed Utopia was just around the corner.

### *Evolution of a Theory*

Darwin's father wanted him to study medicine, and he did so at the University of Edinburgh. But he found this unpalatable and convinced his father to let him study for the ministry. He graduated with a bachelor of arts degree from Cambridge University in 1831.

Darwin was in no hurry to don the robes of a cleric. Though he had no degree in geology or general sciences, he began to do geological surveys with Professors Adam Sedgwick and John Stevens Henslow, with whom he had become close while at Cambridge. Henslow recommended that he sail as a naturalist on the British H.M.S. Beagle on a voyage to Tierra del Fuego and areas in the South Seas, to the Indian Archipelago, and back to England. This voyage began to nourish the intellectual and moral seeds planted by others in the aspiring young naturalist.

Darwin was already exposed to the basic concepts of evolution. Not only his grandfather, but other contemporaries had influenced him. Thomas Malthus, in *An Essay on the Principle of Population*, claimed that there are more offspring produced than can possibly survive because populations tend to remain constant. This suggested to Darwin that when variations within a species occurred, the most useful variation would be the most likely to survive. The idea was eventually expressed as "survival of the fittest."

### *Ancient Earth*

Another major influence on Darwin was Charles Lyell. His *Principles of Geology*, published in 1830, gave Darwin what his budding theory needed — time. Lyell suggested that the earth was ancient and that its present condition was the result of slow, steady changes resulting from processes such as wind, water, and frost. Lyell's theories were radical; lay people as well as scientists had taken Genesis at face value, thereby giving the earth a relatively young age. For Darwin, millions or billions of years of earth history was plenty of time for an infinite number of species to evolve into higher forms.

The five-year trip on the H. M. S. Beagle helped mold Darwin's developing theory that required an old earth. While the crew mapped the South American shoreline, Darwin explored the countryside. He collected specimens of native plants and animals, and bones of extinct animals.

The geology of Patagonia (the extreme southern portion of South America) especially intrigued him. Vast steppe-like plains, including coastal cliffs, were composed of sea shell fragments and sedimentary rocks. This indicated that rock strata had been elevated much higher than the underwater level at which it had been formed. Darwin also observed extensive erosion of volcanic rock. Such evidence confirmed to him an earth that was much older than anything based on biblical information.

Darwin drew the same conclusion from observing species in the Galapagos Archipelago, the "islands of the tortoises." In addition to the giant land tortoises, the islands are home to many lizards and varieties of finches he had not previously seen. Since the islands, formed by volcanic eruptions, are 600 miles west of Peru, the presence of life posed a difficult question: How did everything get to these remote Pacific islands?

Darwin opined that they could have reached the islands by flying or drifting on the water. His high estimation of animals' ability to migrate led to his belief that no special creation was necessary to explain diverse life forms in so many isolated land masses.

## *Natural Selection*

The variations of Galapagos species provided another major impact upon Darwin. The governor of the islands, Nicholas Lawson, claimed that by the shape of a tortoise's shell, he could identify which island the tortoise came from. Fascinated, Darwin began noting differences in life forms on the islands. He confirmed Lawson's observations about the tortoises.

Darwin also found that all the finches were similar except for the size and shape of their beaks. Darwin reasoned that finches that had adapted to seed eating had developed large, heavy beaks for breaking open seeds, while the insect-eating finches had developed small, sharp beaks. This, of course, supposedly exemplified the kind of evolutionary progression, the process of natural selection, that Darwin would spell out in his books. However, if one examines a catalog of modern finches one will notice that different species of finches have very differently shaped beaks. It is clear that the genes for differently shaped beaks are present in the finch family, and Darwin was observing natural selection of variations, a phenomenon which God ordained.

In spite of these modifications of special body parts, such as shells and beaks, the tortoises remained tortoises. The finches remained finches. Even though these kinds had been exposed to what Darwin described as millions of years of isolation and development, there existed a rigid delineation of kinds, no smorgasbord of kinds at varied and different stages of evolution.

But these considerations either did not occur to Darwin or were dismissed. He slowly developed his theory of evolution after he returned to England. He made further observations through studies of domesticated pigeons and by experimental cultivation of plants. He noticed that varieties and sub-varieties differed more from each other if they were raised domestically than if they existed in the wild. Darwin attributed the greater differences among domestic varieties and sub-varieties to the power of selection by man.

As we will see, Gregor Mendel's groundbreaking research on genetics and heredity was still to come, and the full recognition of those discoveries arrived even later. We now know what Darwin didn't: that genes cannot be altered by the conditions of life.

This gap in scientific knowledge, though, was no hindrance to the seeds of evolution that Darwin planted in the fertile intellectual ground of his day. Those seeds were to grow into the pseudo-science that undergirds evolutionary theory to this day.

[1]John Bowlby, *Charles Darwin, A New Life* (New York, London: W.W. Norton and Company, 1990), p. 29.

# The Book

Darwin was stunned.

The views of Alfred Russell Wallace were so close to his. Wallace was still a young naturalist and explorer, yet here he was, formulating a theory of evolution that could upstage Darwin's work.

Darwin's scientist friends Charles Lyell and Joseph Hooper had been encouraging him to publish his fledgling views about natural selection and evolution, but he had delayed. Now Darwin was faced with a manuscript about evolution, sent to him by a fellow British naturalist who wanted an informed opinion.

Darwin's procrastination evaporated in the heat of academic rivalry. He allowed his views, along with Wallace's paper, to be presented to the Linnaean Society in London. Darwin soon published *On the Origin of Species by Means of Natural Selection, or the Preservation of Favoured Races in the Struggle for Life* in 1859.

Some scientists and members of the public received the treatise enthusiastically. Others were shocked. The book disputed the generally accepted view that a separate divine act had created each species. *The Origin of Species* rocked the foundations of biological science and religious thought.

Though that same revolution continues today, it is hard to believe that it began with a book that purported to be scientific, yet fell so short of proving its theories. Darwin wrote extensively about the morphology, instincts, and habits of plants and animals, but his writings failed to include factual confirmation of his theory. Though Darwin's education included medicine, he was not fully trained as a naturalist, and his writings reflect this deficit. Yet he established a pattern in the field of evolution — quasi-science passing for the real thing — that continues to this day. Let's see how Darwin laid the foundation.

### Origin of Species Revisited

When one reads *On the Origin of Species by Means of Natural Selection* today, one is struck by the lack of any real evidence for Darwin's theories. He wrote extensively about the instincts, habits, morphology, etc., of various forms of animal and plant life, but his arguments for evolution are conjecture. Conjecture and argument are well illustrated in his summary of Chapters 12 and 13, entitled "Geographic Distribution."

> In these chapters I have endeavored to show that if we make due allowance for our ignorance of the effects of changes of climate and of the level of the land, which

have certainly occurred within the recent period, and of other changes which have probably occurred, — if we remember how ignorant we are with respect to the many curious means of occasional transport, — if we bear in mind and this is a very important consideration, how often a species may have ranged continuously over a wide area and then have become extinct in the intermediate tracts, — the difficulty is not insuperable in believing that all the individuals of the same species, wherever found, are descended from common parents.[1]

The above paragraph is typical of many of Darwin's arguments. He appeals to ignorance and lack of perfect knowledge to suppress criticism of his theories. Darwin was a remarkable observer and he recognized variation, but he yielded to the tendency to extrapolate to the extreme. It must be recognized that this was a period when men were looking for excuses to cast off authority. The American Revolution had been followed by the French Revolution, and some men chafed under the authority of God as well as men. There was a tendency then, as well as now, for some to accept any explanation for origins which ignored a creator. Even so, his theories were much criticized during his lifetime, and he sought to satisfy his critics in later editions of *The Origin of Species.*

The most serious problem he faced in his day was the recognition of immense gaps in the fossil record. For instance, fossils representing complex life forms were found suddenly appearing in the *Cambrian* geological strata with nothing in the *Precambrian* strata to indicate transitional forms. Darwin answered these challenges with great confidence by assuming that later discoveries would provide missing links. He called this the "imperfection" of the fossil record. The incompleteness of the fossil record was faithfully accepted for about one hundred years. In recent years scientists have become painfully aware that after 130 years of extensive search the fossil record is now considered as complete as it can be expected to be and the gaps persist. The so-called missing links are still missing. There is not one single example of a convincing link between any basic kind and another. Darwin himself admitted in *The Origin of Species*: "Nevertheless, the difficulty of assigning any good reason for the absence of vast piles of strata rich in fossils beneath the Cambrian system is very great . . . and may be truly urged as a valid argument against the views here entertained."[2] And in a later paragraph he said, "The several difficulties here discussed . . . are all of the most serious nature,"[3] and again, "Those who believe that the geological record is in any degree perfect will undoubtedly at once reject the theory."[4] He explains hopefully, "For my part, . . . I look at the geological record as a history of the world imperfectly kept, and written in a changing dialect . . . "[5] The last 130 years of intense searching has produced a record which is now substantially complete. Serious students of origin such as Stephen Jay Gould of Harvard no longer support Darwinian gradual evolution.

As stated earlier, Darwin sought to deal with difficulties of the theory in several chapters of *The Origin of Species*. When viewed critically his answers fall far short of the mark. He saw no difficulty in flying squirrels evolving into bats. He states in Chapter 6 ("Difficulties of the Theory"),

> Although no graduated links of structure, fitted for gliding through the air, now connect the Galeopithecus (flying lemur) with the other Insectivora, yet there is no difficulty in supposing that such links formerly existed, and that each was developed in the same manner as with the less perfectly gliding squirrels; each grade of structure having been useful to its possessor. Nor can I see any insuperable difficulty in further believing that the membrane connected fingers and forearm of the Galeopithecus might have been greatly lengthened by natural selection; and this as far as the organs of flight are concerned, would have converted the animal into a bat.[6]

This simple rationalization of the possible origin of the species as highly and specially developed as the bat cannot be accepted. Darwin passed off the development of the bat from a rodent mammal as a simple progression of variation. The fact is that the origin of the bat is a bona fide mystery.

Bats exhibit several unique physical organs and physiological capabilities. They share with birds and insects the ability to remain airborne for extended periods. Unlike the wings of birds which are covered with feathers which provide aerodynamically efficient contours, the wings of bats are composed chiefly of thin layers of skin stretched over thin bones.

Bats are chiefly nocturnal and are fitted with highly efficient sonar guidance systems. This provides a means of avoiding collision with obstacles and the recognition of their food sources which are mainly flying insects which they feed upon in the dark of night. The orientation sounds which the bats emit are ordinarily above the frequency range which can be heard by the human ear and consist of short clicks. Their ears are extremely sensitive and comparatively large. The brain of a bat is specially developed in the auditory areas, and is capable of rapidly handling and interpreting the auditory signals received. This system outperforms our most advanced radar equipment.

Bats also exhibit extraordinary capabilities to regulate body temperature to suit metabolic needs. Their body temperature is maintained at 100° to 105°F. when fully active. At rest their temperature is allowed to fall, and in sleeping it rapidly falls to that of the surrounding air. Metabolic processes fall with the body temperature, which represents an efficient method of conserving energy.

Darwin knew nothing of DNA, which encodes the structure and functions of life, similar to a computerized language. These unique qualities of the bat which are described would require many highly technical volumes in order to organize and produce such an organism. Darwin was clearly writing from a position of ignorance when he postulated evolution of flying squirrel or lemur to the unique bat. Richard Leakey has written,

"Unfortunately no fossils have yet been found of animals ancestral to the bats."[7]

Darwin exhibits unscientific flights of fancy in a later paragraph when he says,

> Seeing that members of such water-breathing classes as the Crustacea and Mollusca are adapted to live on land and that we have flying birds and mammals, flying insects, and formerly had flying reptiles, it is conceivable that flying fish, which now glide far through the air, slightly rising and turning by the aid of their fluttering fins, might have been modified into perfectly winged animals.[8]

In this statement he gives no scientific evidence of such an hypothesis. He gives no fossil record and he fails to give any evidence explaining how such incredible changes might have occurred. Changes in the DNA code for fish to become bird would be comparable to the revision and addition of hundreds of volumes of intricate scientific instruction for the construction, operation, and reproduction of the organism. This rhetoric might have convinced someone ignorant of our present scientific knowledge 130 years ago, but it is inconceivable that anyone today who is familiar with present knowledge of biological science would accept such material as authoritative.

Under "Organs of Extreme Perfection and Complication" he states,

To suppose that the eye with all its inimitable contrivances for adjusting the focus to different distances, for admitting different amounts of light, and for the correction of spherical and chromatic aberration, could have been formed by natural selection, seems, I freely confess, absurd in the highest degree. When it was first said that the sun stood still and the world turned 'round, the common sense of mankind declared the doctrine false.

Darwin's speculation which follows is not convincing.

It is scarcely possible to avoid comparing the eye with a telescope. We know that this instrument has been perfected by the long-continued efforts of the highest human intellects; and we naturally infer that the eye has been formed by a somewhat analogous process. But may not this inference be presumptuous? Have we any right to assume that the Creator works by intellectual powers like those of man? If we must compare the eye to an optical instrument, we ought in imagination to take a thick layer of transparent tissues, with spaces filled with fluid, and with a nerve sensitive to light beneath, and then suppose every part of this layer to be continually changing slowly in density, so as to separate into layers of different densities and thicknesses, placed at different distances from each other, and with the surfaces of each layer slowly changing in form. Further, we must suppose that there is the power, represented by natural selection or the survival of the fittest, always intently watching each slight alteration in the transparent layers; and carefully preserving each which, under varied circumstances, in any way or in any degree, tends to produce a distincter image. . . . And may we not believe that a living optical instrument might thus be formed as superior to one of glass, as the works of the Creator are to those of man?[9]

One wonders if his imagination would have led him so far if he had known the eye is said to be able to handle a million bits of information per second and pass this on to the brain, where highly complex connections exist with ramifications into the conscious centers allowing appreciation of the information transmitted.

In another section, Darwin writes, "If it could be demonstrated that any complex organ existed which could not possibly have been formed by numerous, successive, slight modification my theory would absolutely break down. But I can find out no such case."[10] He then describes his presumption of a remarkable transition of swimbladder to lung, a presumption which has been shown to be quite incorrect. I quote Darwin:

> All physiologists admit that the swimbladder is homologous, or 'ideally similar' in position and structure with the lungs of the higher vertebrate animals: hence there is no reason to doubt that the swimbladder has actually been converted into lungs, or an organ used exclusively for respiration. According to this view it may be inferred that all vertebrate animals with true lungs are descended by ordinary generation from an ancient or unknown prototype, which was furnished with a floating apparatus or swimbladder.[11]

We see him adamantly "finding out no such case" and in his "proof" being absolutely wrong scientifically. It has been demonstrated quite conclusively the swimbladder did not evolve into lungs. He thus proves to the contrary that his theory breaks down.

The eye is found in different forms in mammals, insects, and in the octopus with no evidence of development from another lower species, and with no connecting links with these various species. This would seem to be another such example.

He admits:

The electric organs of fishes offer a special difficulty: for it is impossible to conceive by what steps these wondrous organs have been produced. We do not know of what use they are. In the Gymnotus and Torpedo they serve as powerful means of defense, and perhaps for securing prey; yet in the Ray an analogous organ in the tail manifests so little electricity, even when the animal is greatly irritated that it can hardly be of any use for these purposes. It is generally admitted that there exists between these organs and ordinary muscle a close analogy, in that muscular contraction is accompanied by an electrical discharge. Beyond this we cannot at present go in the way of explanation; but it would be extremely bold to maintain that no transitions are possible by which these organs might have been gradually developed.

These organs appear at first to offer another and far more serious difficulty: for they occur in about a dozen kinds of fish, of which several are widely remote in their affinities. When the same organ is found in several members of the same class, we may generally attribute its presence to inheritance from a common ancestor. But we see in the several fishes provided with electrical organs that these are situated in different parts of the body, that they differ in construction, as in the arrangement of the plates, and in the process by which the electricity is excited, and lastly in being supplied with nerves proceeding from different sources. Consequently, there is no reason to suppose that they had been inherited from a common progenitor; for had this been the case they would have closely resembled each other in all respects. Thus the difficulty of an organ, apparently the same, arising in several remotely allied species disappears, leaving only the lesser difficulty, namely by what steps these organs have been developed in each group of fishes.[12]

Thus Darwin ends the discussion about electrical organs, leaving the difficulty unanswered, but claiming to be left with only a lesser difficulty. It would seem that the difficulty encountered arises from the fact that God has conceived of concepts, and has implemented these concepts in various ways, for various purposes in different living organisms. As with other concepts of God, man has difficulty explaining them unless he recognizes God as the ultimate cause. Concepts require intelligence. The theory of evolution by definition absolutely and unconditionally requires thoughtless change by chance alone.

In this same chapter ("Difficulties of the Theory"), Darwin discusses fertilization methods of various plants. His description of the incredible contrivance of the orchid, *Coryanthes,* is interesting when one considers the fact that Darwin is here claiming that this somehow came into being by pure chance with no plan and for no purpose. To quote Darwin:

This orchid has part of its labellum or lower lip hollowed out into a great bucket into which drops of almost pure water continually fall from two secreting horns:

and when the bucket is half full the water overflows by a spout on one side. The basal part of the labellum stands over the bucket, and is itself hollowed out into a sort of chamber with two lateral entrances; within this chamber there are curious fleshy ridges. Crowds of large humble bees (bumble bees) visit the gigantic flowers of this orchid not to suck nectar but to gnaw off the ridges within the chambers; in doing this they frequently push each other into the bucket, and their wings being thus wetted they cannot fly away, but are compelled to crawl out through the passage formed by the overflow. The passage is narrow and is roofed over by the column, so that a bee, in forcing its way out, first rubs its back against the viscid stigma and then against the viscid glands of the pollen-masses. The pollen-masses are thus glued to the back of the bee which first happens to crawl out through the passage of the lately expanded flower. When the bee, thus provided, flies to another flower and is pushed into the bucket and then crawls out by the passage, the pollen-mass comes first in contact with the viscid stigma and adheres to it and the flower is fertilized. Now at last we see the full use of every part of the flower.[13]

Knowing nothing of the intricacies of the DNA code nor of the many contrivances maintaining stability of phenotype, he says of Coryanthes:

How in the foregoing instances can we understand the graduated scale of complexity and the multifarious means for gaining the same end? The answer is that when two forms vary, which already differ from each other, the variability will not be the same, and the results obtained through natural selection for the same general purpose will not be the same. Every highly developed organism has passed through many changes, and each modification may be again and again altered. Hence the structure of each part of each species is the sum of many inherited changes.[14]

In this statement, I see no explanation of how Coryanthes came to possess such a complex system of pollination. Other flowers are quite successful in pollination without such complex mechanisms. Darwin believed in his theory and caused everything to be explained by reciting it. As before, there is no recitation of hereditary steps through which Coryanthes passed to arrive at this extraordinary system of pollination.

In Chapter 7 of *Origin of Species*, Darwin attempts to answer miscellaneous objections to the theory of natural selection. He says,

> A distinguished zoologist, Mr. St. George Mivart, has recently collected all the objections which have ever been advanced against the theory of selection, as propounded by Mr. Wallace and myself, and has illustrated them with admirable art and force. When thus marshalled, they make a formidable array . . . .[15]

One of the objections raised by Mr. Mivart concerned mammary glands. Mammary glands are absolutely indispensable in the rearing of young mammals, and without perfectly functioning mammary glands the newborn would surely die. No newborn can possibly survive without an adequate supply of mother's milk, unless it is artificially supplied by an intelligent being. Mr. Mivart asks, "Is it conceivable that the young of any animal was ever saved from destruction by accidentally sucking a drop of scarcely nutritious fluid from an accidentally *hypertrophied cutaneous* gland of its mother? And even if one was so, what chance was there of the perpetuation of such a variation?"[16] This is an important question, which would require a direct answer. In his reply to this criticism, Mr. Darwin failed to offer a reasonable step by step path of the development of the breast, but offers the following:

> The development of the mammary glands would have been of no service unless the young were able to partake of the secretion. There is no greater difficulty in understanding how young mammals have instinctively learned to suck the breast, than in understanding how unhatched chickens have learned to break the egg shell by tapping against it with their beaks.[17]

Thus, he explained how young animals learned to suckle by comparing suckling to the equally unexplained phenomenon of chicks pecking their way out of egg shells! This explanation may have sufficed to convince men of science who were looking for an alternative to Creation, but it would appear most proponents and teachers of Darwin's theory had neglected to read his book, and had not had an opportunity to judge how unscientifically he rationalized his theory.

In *The Origin of Species* Darwin failed to satisfactorily answer the many objections to his theory which had previously been raised. As we will learn in Chapter 8, many of the leading evolutionists of the present day are unable to accept Darwin's theory of gradual evolution by means of natural selection of variations. For instance, the fossil record fails to demonstrate kinds gradually evolving into other kinds. These evolutionists note the sudden appearance of numerous fully formed species with no previous forms from which they might be evolved. "Punctuated Equilibrium," the theory proposed by Professor Stephen Jay Gould of Harvard and Dr. Niles Eldredge, Curator of Invertebrate Paleontology at the American Museum of Natural History, recognizes the fact that species tend to remain unchanged and that new species appear suddenly, perfectly formed and adapted to the environment. Darwin has this to say about such prospects:

> He who believes that some ancient form was transformed suddenly through an internal force or tendency into, for instance, one furnished with wings, will be almost compelled to assume, in opposition to all analogy, that many individuals were buried simultaneously . . . He will further be compelled to believe that many structures beautifully adapted to all the other parts of the same creature and to the surrounding conditions, have been suddenly produced; and of such complex and wonderful co-adaptations, he will not be able to assign a shadow of an explanation. He will be forced to admit that these great and sudden transformations have left no trace of their action on the embryo. To admit all this is as it seems to me, to enter into the realms of miracle and to leave those of Science.[18]

Darwin and I agree on this point.

[1] Charles Darwin, *The Origin of Species by Means of Natural Selection* (New York: A. L. Burt Company, Publishers, 1909), p. 424.

[2] Ibid., pp. 339-340.

[3] Ibid., pp. 341-342.

[4] Ibid., p. 342.

[5] Ibid.

[6] Ibid., p. 166.

[7] Richard E. Leakey, *The Illustrated Origin of Species* by Charles Darwin, Abridged and Introduced by Richard E. Leakey (New York: Hill and Wang, 1979), p. 128.

[8] Ibid., p. 106.

[9] Ibid., p. 111.

[10] Ibid., p. 112.

[11] Ibid., p. 113.

[12] Ibid., p. 114.

[13] Ibid., p. 115.

[14] Ibid., p. 116.

[15] Ibid., p. 122.

[16] Ibid., p. 126.

[17] Ibid.

[18] Ibid., p. 129.

# The Self-Made Watch

The camera pans the African plain. A flock of birds rises up from the lake, leaving a small group of gazelles cautiously drinking at the shore. A British voice describes an approaching cheetah, slinking through the tall grass.

You squinch a bit as the cheetah, after running down its prey, sinks its fatal bite into the gazelle's neck. (You also fail to note the narrator's discreet plug for Darwin as he rhapsodizes about the "wilderness code" as "survival of the fittest.") But if it is the gazelle's pain that stirs you, your empathy may be wasted. Studies of human pain reveal that people (and apparently animals) frequently feel no immediate pain when they are injured. We know that much of the pain related to violence is blocked by opiates produced in our bodies.

How does our body know to respond in this way? What triggers this involuntary production of special opiates? Could such a miraculous, complex analgesic system have been produced by chance simply through changes between generations?

Such knowledge of the body's systems was relatively infantile in Darwin's day. But what was lacking in empirical evidence was substituted through Darwin's conjecture and in public debate. Darwin's budding theory of evolution excited the brightest minds in America and England, and eventually in the rest of Europe.

Scant research may have prevented a more specified track for debate on countless quandaries raised by Darwinism, such as how the body's system of pain relief could have evolved. Still, the big thinkers of Darwin's era were willing to tackle a broader philosophical dilemma posed by evolutionary theory: Does life progress upward by itself, or does its complexity and variation prove the action of a divine hand? The issue was no more settled in the nineteenth century than it is in the twentieth, but the arguments bear examination. Just as Elijah challenged the people on Mount Carmel: There are two stark opinions. Choose one.

### *Locking Horns*

One of Darwin's biggest cheerleaders was zoologist and atheist Sir Thomas Henry Huxley. Because he so fiercely and successfully championed the theory of evolution in debates, he became known as "Darwin's Bulldog."

One of Darwin's staunchest opponents was the Anglican bishop of Oxford, Samuel Wilberforce. A professor of mathematics at Oxford, Wilberforce did not stand up well to the assaults of Huxley and other specialists in the life sciences, but his wit and charm embellished the rhetorical skills he employed to rebut the faddish philosophy of the day. Known as "Soapy Sam," Wilberforce was a popular speaker who tried to present the church's opinion in opposition to Darwin's ideas.

During a debate between Darwin's Bulldog and Soapy Sam, recounted in a lecture by Dr. A. E. Wilder-Smith,[1] Bishop Wilberforce relied on the self-evident truth that a watch requires a watchmaker. No machine makes itself, including a living body, or even a cell. This was known as Paley's "Natural Theology," as expressed in a book of the same name published in 1802. Paley's common-sense theory was widely accepted at the time and still makes sense.

Huxley countered by appealing to the Probability Law: When time is infinity, probability equals 1, or certainty. In eternity, anything can — and will — happen. Huxley argued that if six apes typed on typewriters for eternity, eventually the Twenty-third Psalm would appear in their reams of trash, purely by chance. If a psalm could be formed by random happenings, so could a man. Huxley thereby replaced the Creator with Chance.

Much of the scientific community to this day holds to Huxley's argument, though it does not withstand scrutiny for two major reasons.

First, look at a crucial juncture in the theory of evolution — the spontaneous origin of life. In his lecture, Dr. Wilder-Smith explained that all organic chemical reactions are reversible. For example, if an amino acid, a compound critical to life, were to form in a watery solution, it would quickly dissolve. Such a compound must be separated from the solution or protected from becoming unformed by some special process requiring intelligent intervention.

How does this compare to the tireless typing of apes? Instead of accumulating stacks of paper filled with gibberish, the typists would never get past the first character. They could bang their keyboards into eternity, but their typewriter ribbons would be filled with disappearing ink. Just as the aspiring life in the water solution would not last to evolve or even reproduce, the monkey's letters would, in effect, disappear long before they ever got as far as "The Lord is my shepherd."

A second major problem with Huxley's argument is that the earth is not infinitely old. Although some of the older dating methods suggest the earth may be as much as 4.5 billion years old, other methods of guesswork fail to support an age of more than thousands of years. None put a dent in eternity. Consequently, when it comes to the formation of life, nature has not had the luxury of infinity to mix molecule cocktails and see which ones squirm. The same difficulty arises, as we will see in a later chapter, when you consider probabilities regarding mutations by which species allegedly moved up the evolutionary ladder.

Furthermore, paleontologists and the Genesis Creation account agree in a very broad sense that life appeared relatively soon after earth was made. This means the period in which life emerged was even more restricted than the earth's reputed age of five billion years. The closer one examines the probabilities behind evolutionary theory, the more it begins to look like a miracle of greater proportion than the Genesis account.

## Pain's Gain

Let us return to the principles of pain. They illustrate both superficial problems with evolution, as well as philosophic weaknesses evident in Darwin's approach to science, life, and religion.

Darwin's theory was partly based on the idea that pain, suffering, and death over many generations — the grisly realities of survival of the fittest — produced the wonders of biology. Yet to Darwin, the atrocious behavior that produced these horrors of nature could not be reconciled with a loving Creator. After all, why would a compassionate, all-powerful God allow suffering?

Darwin was mistaken on three key counts. First, he rejected the Genesis teaching that he had been fully exposed to in college: that suffering and death entered the world with man's sin. Their existence in no way contradicts the nature of God. Darwin failed to recognize

God's power and desire to reconcile all things, including suffering.

Secondly, Darwin did not fully appreciate the extent to which God had provided for the relief of pain and suffering by biological mechanisms which we partially understand today. Nine opiate-type substances have been identified in the brain and spinal cord. They act on the analgesic — or pain-relieving — system. One of the principal substances, *dynorphin*, packs two hundred times the effectiveness of morphine. Another one, *endorphin*, is released in large quantities during periods of acute stress. It takes a great leap of evolutionary faith to imagine the process by which our bodies might have formed these agents by chance, and by which they are released when needed. Much more sensible is the proposition that a compassionate God instilled them in His creation.

The third point which Darwin apparently failed to grasp was the positive role that pain plays in our welfare. Not only Darwin, but few others stop to realize the wonder of the built-in alarm system God put into our bodies. Our brain translates the casserole dish burning our hand as pain. What better way to get our attention and prevent further damage to our skin? Pain lets us know if our skin has been exposed to too much sun at the beach, or if the stack of lumber we're carrying is about to shred the skin on our palms.

Pain, then, is a multi-faceted aspect of humans and

animals. Its existence, as well as the nervous system, the spinal cord, and the brain, not to mention the analgesic system's production of opiate-like substances, astounds anyone who studies the body. One must summon a mountain of faith in chance to believe that random changes in species led to such an assemblage. No evolutionist has come close to demonstrating the mechanisms by which pain and its related systems have developed in vertebrates.

### Order versus Disorder

Let's return to Paley's argument that a watch needs a watchmaker. This was no mere sophistry on his part, but an expression of the flip side of what we know to be a fundamental scientific principle — *the second law of thermodynamics*.

The law states that everything progresses toward a state of increasing disorganization. *Entropy* — a measure of that disorder — constantly increases. Even if your house is well-insulated, you have to keep running the heater because the warmth seeps out. Look at the best-made machines. Even they will wear out some day. Try as hard as they may, inventors have never produced a perpetual motion machine because they cannot escape the mandate of the second law, which insists that energy will escape from a system.

What is true on the macro level is also true on the micro level. There is no scientific basis to expect carbon, hydrogen, and oxygen atoms to oppose the second law by combining in ways that suddenly create life, and therefore energy. Likewise, one would not expect the miraculously formed microorganisms to naturally progress to higher states of order and energy as they climb the evolutionary ladder.

The uniformity of the second law gives every reason to expect just the opposite — increasing disarray. Life, after all, is a struggle against disorder, against the forces of aging, that threaten to render an organism lifeless, subject then to rapid entropy in the form of decay.

When Paley and Wilberforce argued that a watch requires a watchmaker, they assumed the natural state of disorder in the universe. They knew that overcoming the natural tendency toward chaos would require an outside hand, a higher being. No amount of shaking, compression, or strikes of lightning would turn gears and springs into a watch. Even six immortal monkeys with tiny screwdrivers and eyeglasses would not do it. Only a watchmaker could.

### Passing the Torch

In the last paragraph of *The Origin of Species*, Darwin referred to the Creator as having originally breathed life into a few forms, or maybe into one. Today, someone holding that view would be considered a theistic evolutionist — believing that God was the creator of life, but that he used evolution to bring about the many species we see today. I, too, once fell into that camp.

In view of his later writings, it is doubtful that Darwin believed in a divine Creator, and perhaps he was merely employing semantics to mollify the many believing scientists and lay readers of his day. He was, after all, hesitant to suggest that man was descended from apes, fearing that such propositions might add to the prejudices against his theories. His worries, though, did not stop him from publishing *The Descent of Man* in 1870. This work continued his early pattern of conjecture, failing to produce the evidence needed to show how man could have descended from apes. To knowledgeable students of evolution, the book is an embarrassment.

As to whether Darwin's beliefs about a Creator grew or diminished by the end of his life, there are conflicting accounts. For over fifty years claims have been made that he accepted Christianity toward the end of his life. One account which was circulated under the title "Darwin's Last Hours" quoted an English evangelist, "Lady Hope," as claiming that he asked her to speak to his servants and some neighbors about "Christ Jesus — and His Salvation." In a book edited by Emmett L. Williams, and written by Professor Wilbert H. Rusch and John W. Klotz[2] evidence is cited completely denying the authenticity of this report. Darwin characterized himself as an agnostic, a development resulting from abandonment of his faith in the authority of Scripture. It would appear that Darwin's spiritual belief was caught in the snare of his own theory, a significant danger for all who accept the teachings of evolution as truth.

[1]A. E. Wilder-Smith, D. Sc., Ph. D. , Dr. es. Sc., F. R. I. C., in lecture, "The Creation-Evolution Controversy" at Friendship Baptist Church, Raleigh, NC, May 15, 1984.

[2]Wilbert H. Rusch, Sr. and John W. Klotz, Edited by Emmett L. Williams, *Did Charles Darwin Become a Christian?* (5093 Williamsport Drive, Norcross, Georgia 30092, Creation Research Society Books, 1988), pp. 12, 13, 37, 38.

# Variations

Darwin's theory is based upon the selection of variations by natural processes with the resultant appearance of superior varieties. The accumulation of improved varieties, according to his theory, has manifested itself in the gradual evolution of more complex and more perfect species. Darwin stated in Chapter 6 of *Origin of Species*, "If it could be demonstrated that any complex organ existed, which could not possibly have been formed by numerous, successive, slight modifications, my theory would absolutely break down." In Chapter 4 several such instances were discussed. These included the eye, the swimbladder of fishes, the electric organs of fishes and the orchid, Coryanthes. There are many other such instances, including the human brain, with the ability to utilize language for communication, and the development of the various organ systems such as heart and circulation, kidney, liver, etc.

One of the most striking examples of a development which could not possibly have evolved is the source of individual minor variation itself. This is the invention and creation of sexual reproduction through which every individual is unique and unlike any other individual. It is typical of God's way.

The simplest known self-sustaining organisms are bacteria and blue-green algae. These are called *prokaryotes* and do not contain a cell nucleus. They reproduce by simple cell division called mitosis. In this reproductive process the chromosomes and the cells simply divide and the original single cell becomes two. Thus the unicelled organism is cloned. In this process each new individual is ordinarily exactly like its parent. No variation occurs unless a mutation of the chromosome occurs, and in a later chapter we will learn that mutations are almost always detrimental. Given a variety of bacteria, one bacterium is in most respects like another.

Organisms which reproduce sexually are known as *eukaryotes*, and include all plants and animals except prokaryotes. The cell body of eukaryotes contains a nucleus within which the genetic material (*chromosomes*) is located. Reproduction is accomplished through a much more complicated process and involves male and female. During the reproductive process one-half of the genetic material provided for the offspring is supplied by the male and one-half is supplied by the female.

It should be obvious to anyone that sexual reproduction is basically much more complicated and requires much greater energy utilization than prokaryotic cloning. This is especially noteworthy among our feathered friends and among other animal varieties which spend a great deal of time and energy in courtship and the rearing of the young. Sexual reproduction, as contrasted with asexual cloning (mitosis) is a time of considerable vulnerability and could not be looked upon as a chance evolutionary advance leading to more efficient reproduction. It can only be viewed as another of God's plans.

Roger Y. Stanier, microbiologist with the Institute Pasteur, Paris, France, stated:

> . . . the structural differences between eukaryotic and prokaryotic cells are expressive of highly important differences in the way that universal cell functions are accomplished: notably the transmission and expression of genetic information, the performance of energy metabolism, and the entry and exit of materials. It is evident that the line of demarcation between eukaryotic and prokaryotic cellular organisms is the largest and most profound single evolutionary discontinuity in the contemporary biological world.[1]

Elsewhere Dr. Stanier has indicated there are no intermediates. In other words, eukaryotes appeared quite independently of prokaryotes and both groups of organisms went on to flourish. There is no rational way one system could have evolved into another and no plausible reason, except to establish individuality and variation. In it, one can recognize God's ultimate plan for human marriage.

Careful thought about many special features of various organisms will lead the reader to question how evolution could possibly account for the wide variety of physical characteristics, physiological devices and the instincts which are exhibited. The more one studies the various forms of life, the more one is struck by the infinite variety and the incredible uniqueness of individuals. Darwin and others have seized upon an invention of our Creator to challenge His creativeness, and to claim as the creating force this wonderful quality of life which He instilled. We are reminded of what Paul said in Romans 1:20-23a:

> For the invisible things of him from the creation of the world are clearly seen, being understood by the things that are made, even his eternal power and Godhead; so that they are without excuse: Because that, when they knew God, they glorified him not as God, neither were thankful; but became vain in their imaginations, and their foolish heart was darkened. Professing themselves to be wise, they became fools, and changed the glory of the incorruptible God . . . .

Relatively minor variations among kinds appear to be possible by mutations. When a cell reproduces, the genes are copied and become the blueprint of the new cell. Although there are many safeguards which have been created to avoid instances of imperfect translation of genes during the replication process of DNA, occasional mistakes occur. Evolutionists Bruce Wallace of Cornell University and Theodosius Dobzhansky of Columbia University, experts in the field of mutations, point out that "a mutant gene is essentially an incomplete, imperfect defective copy of the parent gene."[2] Writing about mutations of *Drosophila* or fruit fly, they say, "The more radical the change, the less likely it is to be harmless, not to speak of its being useful. Yet, mutants do occur which make the fly a little bit larger or smaller, develop a little faster or more slowly, have slightly more or fewer bristles on certain parts of the body, deposit on the average slightly more or fewer eggs."[3]

Evolutionists claim that the variations produced by mutations are the building blocks of evolution. Thus, they see mutations resulting in improved genes. Mutations which involve major functional or morphologic characteristics seriously interfere with vigor and reproduction, and many are lethal. In general, they produce monstrosities and would not be expected to be proper building blocks for the creation of improved species.

In this regard, Wallace and Dobzhansky say: "You would hardly expect a masterpiece, such as a painting by El Greco or Rembrandt, to be improved if some dauber took it upon himself to change it. Mutation spoils a gene much more often than it improves it for exactly the same reasons."[4] Regarding the dangers of radiation to living organisms, they maintain "since most mutations cause some damage to their carriers, increased mutations means increased damage." There has been much written about the dangers of radiation-induced mutations to mankind, but no one has yet claimed any possible benefit. The useful mutants selected by breeders of agricultural plants does not contradict this statement. The useful mutants represent a tiny residue selected from a much greater mass of mutants, most of which are useless or harmful. Many of the useful ones fail to reproduce themselves and must be artificially produced in each generation. Most would fail to compete in the wild with natural varieties.[5] Their usefulness is dependent upon special characteristics beneficial to man or to special environmental situations.

We are all familiar with similar kinds of plants and animals in the wild which exhibit differences in size, coloring, and other characteristics. Darwin was much impressed by the varying finches on Galapagos. We see differences in various breeds of seagulls and ducks. There is no way of knowing how much of this variation is due to special creation and how much is due to mutation. Because of the fact that mutation is a defective copy of an existing gene, it makes no sense that an improved gene can result from an accidental, chance, non-intelligent error in transcription. Indeed, evolutionists consider "survival of the fittest" a route to improved species, when experience shows it is a phenomenon which works to prevent decline of a species. There is no evidence that gazelles run faster now than they ran 6,000 years ago. Wildlife managers are very much aware that herds of animals decline when natural forces cease to work to weed out weak specimens. The ecological battle of nature is for maintenance of standards, not progressive alteration to higher forms.

An interesting method of variation exists among bacteria and perhaps some fungi through the action of plasmids. *Plasmids* are bits of genetic units which are known to affect chromosomes (DNA) of bacteria. They are especially important in the transfer of antibiotic resistance. This aspect of the influence of plasmids has been extensively studied in E. coli, the common bacterium of the human colon. The genetic material of plasmids is very specific for a particular antibiotic, and this genetic information can be passed by them from one group of bacteria to another. Determinates for resistance to seven different antibiotics are known to be carried by specific plasmids. They are similar to viruses by being dependent on living cells to replicate and to function. Obviously, the unicelled organization of bacteria and close proximity of one organism to another in colonies allows free access of these particles to cross between individuals.

Resistance to penicillins and the newer cephalosporins is due to the production of penicillinase or *Beta-lactamase*, an enzyme which destroys the antibiotic. This enzyme is produced by the genetic code inserted into the genome (DNA) of the bacteria by the plasmid. Technically, the bacteria furnished with this new information can be considered to be mutants, but this mutation is not produced by an accidental or chance error of transcription. The information is widely distributed among naturally resistant bacteria and does not represent some new invention by chance. Unfortunately, many scientists have misinterpreted this phenomenon and lump this type of mutation with the transcription errors. Penicillinase is a very complex protein enzyme which cannot be produced by any man-made laboratory. It cannot be produced by a bacterium through an accident. The blueprint must be furnished by plasmids.

The original genetic information for the production of penicillinase did not originate in response to contact with penicillin. Bacteria resistant to antibiotics which were developed more than 120 years later have been cultured from the bodies of seamen who died during an arctic expedition in 1848. In fact, there are many bacteria which are naturally resistant to most antibiotics. Bacterial resistance involves not only the production of enzymes which destroy the antibiotic, but cell membranes which fail to absorb the antibiotic. The genetic information distributed from one bacterium to another by plasmids cannot be imagined to cause an evolution to a higher form of bacteria. It is simply information widely scattered throughout the bacterial kingdom, and the mutated bacterium remains a bacterium.

We have seen that variation is a regular occurrence among sexually reproducing eukaryotes which includes man and an occasional occurrence among asexually reproducing prokaryotes which includes bacteria and blue-green algae. The regular individuality of eukaryotes can be visualized as God's design to make us all unique and allow adjustments to changing and different environmental pressures. There is nothing scientifically shown to suggest that variation provides a mechanism for the progressive evolution of one class of organism to another, or the development of a complex organ such as the eye or the brain.

Darwin might be forgiven for having imagined an exaggerated potential for normal variations, but modern knowledge should put the concept to rest.

[1]Roger Y. Stanier, Edward A. Adelburg, John L. Ingraham, Mark L. Wheelis, *Introduction to the Microbial World* (Englewood Cliffs, NJ: Prentice-Hall, 1979), p. 46.

[2]Bruce Wallace and Theodosius Dobzhansky, *Radiation, Genes, and Man: Biological Aspects of Radiation Hazards* (New York: Holt, Rinehart & Winston, 1963), p. 45.

[3]Ibid., pp. 45-46.

[4]Ibid., p. 45.

[5]Ibid., p. 49.

# Paleontology's "Trade Secret"

It was just an ordinary day in 1938, in the Indian Ocean off Cape Province in South Africa. Then, 1,640 feet below the surface, a fish made a mistake. It also made history.

The fish that wandered into a fisherman's net was a coelacanth. It was special for two reasons:

(1) It was thought to have exited earth 90 million years ago, based on fossil records.

(2) A close prehistoric relative of the coelacanth was thought to have been an intermediate species between fish and amphibians. Why hadn't this coelacanth evolved into something else by now?

Scientists compared this survivor with the records of its ancestors and found it was basically unchanged. No mutations. No sign of flopping its way up the evolutionary ladder. Other coelacanths have been caught since, thousands of miles from the 1938 find. None have supported what until then had been evolutionary "fact," that this group of fishes represented an important link between fishes and amphibia and other terrestrial vertebrates.

## *Fossil Fantasies*

"It ain't so much the things we don't know that get us in trouble," said American humorist Artemus Ward, "It's the things we know that ain't so."

That the concept of an evolving coelacanth "ain't so" was no great surprise to anyone who had demanded adequate proof for evolution. The discovery of the coelacanth merely added to the weight of evidence against evolution already shown — or not shown — by the fossil record. There was no fossil of evolving coelacanths because none were evolving to begin with.

Darwin's faith in his theory rested largely on a firm belief that the fossil record would demonstrate transitional forms proving slow evolutionary change from simple organisms to the complex. He was firmly aware of the lack of supportive evidence in the fossil record as it existed in his day. After over one hundred and thirty years the record is considered complete and no transitional forms have been uncovered which might support his theory.

In 1859, over 130 years ago, Darwin wrote in Chapter 10 of *The Origin of Species*,

> The abrupt manner in which whole groups of species suddenly appear in certain formations has been urged as a fatal objection to the belief in the transmutation of species. If numerous species belonging to the same genera or families have really started into life at once, the

fact would be fatal to the theory of evolution through natural selection. For the development of a group of forms, all descended from one progenitor, must have been an extremely slow process; and the progenitors must have lived long before their modified descendants. But we continually overrate the perfection of the geological record . . . .[1]

In 1965, one hundred and six years later, A. G. Fischer wrote: "The base of the Cambrian period is marked in marine sediments around the world by the appearance of an abundant animal life . . . This sudden appearance of diverse animal stocks has been the most vexing riddle in paleontology."[2]

In 1980, one hundred and twenty-one years after Darwin made excuses for the failure of the fossil record to support evolution, Stephen Gould of Harvard said:

Today the modern synthesis of evolution is being challenged in almost every respect by scientists. The synthetic theory (Darwin's) is no longer adequate to explain evolution in spite of its persistence in textbook orthodoxy. The living world was not constructed as a smooth and seamless continuum permitting simple extrapolation from the lowest to the highest level.

Everybody knows the fossil record doesn't provide much evidence for gradualism; it is full of gaps and discontinuities. These gaps are all attributed to the notorious imperfections of the record, but this is not an adequate explanation. The fossil record shows one thing which cannot be attributed to its imperfections; most species don't change. They may get a little bigger or bumpier but they remain the same species. This remarkable stasis has generally been ignored. If it doesn't agree with your ideas, you don't talk about it . . . Gradual change is not the normal state of the species but rather stasis and discontinuity are normal.[3]

Many evolutionists still claim the theory of Darwin which Stephen Jay Gould refers to as gradualism is by this time proved by the fossil record. This is nonsense. Gould has also stated,

> The extreme rarity of transitional forms in the fossil record persists as the trade secret of paleontology — Darwin's argument still persists as the favored escape of most paleontologists from the embarrassment of a record that seems to show so little of evolution directly — it was never 'seen' in the rocks.[4]

Gould and Fischer are not alone in admitting the fossil record fails to substantiate evolution.

G. G. Simpson, paleontologist of Columbia University, wrote: "The regular absence of transitional forms is not confined to mammals, but is an almost universal phenomenon, *as has long been noted by paleontologists* [emphasis mine]."[5]

T. Storer (zoologist) has said: "The real origin of horses is unknown."[6] This statement is confirmed by Dr. Niles Eldredge of the American Museum in New York, NY. Yet, the famous "Horse Series" appears in many textbooks of biology as an authoritative example of evolution.

Professor E.J.H. Corner of the Cambridge University Botany School wrote in 1961:

> I still think that to the unprejudiced, the fossil record of plants is in favor of special creation. If, however, another explanation could be found . . . it would be the knell of the theory of evolution. Can you imagine how an orchid, a duckweed, and a palm have come from the same ancestry, and have we any evidence for this assumption? The evolutionists must be prepared with an answer, but I think that most would break down before an inquisition.[7]

Evolutionists claim fish evolved into amphibia, but no intermediates have been found despite diligent search. This is characteristic of all major classes of animals. D. M. Raup and S. M. Stanley wrote in 1971: "Unfortunately, the origins of most higher categories are shrouded in mystery; commonly new higher categories appear abruptly in the fossil record without evidence of transitional forms."[8]

H. Smith stated regarding the evolution of vertebrates, "The gap remains unbridged and the best place to start the evolution of the vertebrates is in the imagination."[9] In a similar vein W. E. Swinton of the British Museum of Natural History said of the origin of birds that it was largely a matter of deduction, because there was no fossil of the stages through which the remarkable change from reptile to bird was achieved.[10]

Despite these many denials by experts in their respective fields, evolutionists claim and teach that the fossil record "proves" evolution to be a fact.

Luther D. Sunderland, B.S., an aerospace engineer with the General Electric Company, has spent many years studying the scientific evidences of theories of origins. Several years ago he assisted the New York State Board of Regents in a study of how theories on origins should be presented in a revised version of the state's Regents Biology Syllabus. Mr. Sunderland interviewed five leading paleontologists associated with several of the leading natural history museums of the world, all of which contain large fossil collections. Those interviewed were: Dr. Niles Eldredge, curator of Invertebrate Paleontology at the American Museum in New York, NY; Dr. David M. Raup, curator of Geology at the Field Museum of Natural History in Chicago, IL; Dr. David Pilbeam, former curator of the Peabody Museum of Natural History at Yale and later professor of Anthropology at Harvard; Dr. Donald Fisher, state paleontologist at the New York State Natural History Museum; and Dr. Colin Patterson, a senior paleontologist at the British Museum of Natural History. The results of these interviews were recorded in an interesting book written by Mr. Sunderland entitled *Darwin's Enigma: Fossils and Other Problems*.[11]

Mr. Sunderland records that Dr. Raup had previously published an article in the Field Museum journal entitled "Conflicts Between Darwinism and Paleontology" which stated that the 250,000 species of plants and animals recorded and deposited in museums throughout the world did not support Darwin's theories.[12] He also asserts that Dr. Colin Patterson wrote in a letter to Mr. Sunderland that he did not know of any real evidence of evolutionary transitions either among living or fossilized organisms.[13]

Mr. Sunderland summarized the opinions of these experts as follows: "None of the five museum officials could offer a single example of a transitional series of fossilized organisms that would document the transformation of one basically different type to another."[14] He also pointed out that evolutionists tend to consider the theory untestable, and the only limitation on imagination in constructing evolutionary scenarios was the gullibility level of the public. For instance, Dr. Eldredge is quoted as saying that there are some people who are fed up with "imaginary stories" that have been written about the nature of the history of life. He also said:

> I admit that an awful lot of that has gotten into the textbooks as though it were true. For instance, the most famous example still on exhibit downstairs (in the American Museum) is the exhibit on horse evolution prepared perhaps 50 years ago. That has been presented as literal truth in textbook after textbook. Now I think that is lamentable, particularly because the people who propose these kinds of stories themselves may be aware of the speculative nature of some of the stuff. But by the time it filters down to the textbooks, we've got science as truth and we've got a problem.[15]

This complete failure of the fossil record to support evolution will undoubtedly come as a shock to the average reader. We have been led to believe by our teachers and by writings in current journals and newspaper articles that the fossil record authoritatively confirms the theory of evolution. This is an absolute deception and those who maintain that it does are either ignorant of the facts or are deluded by their preconceptions.

The bird is commonly claimed to have developed from reptiles. Yet, in *Avian Biology*, Vol. 1, there appears the following admission:

> The living birds are the best known group of animals, but their origin, history, and phylogeny are very poorly documented in comparison with the other vertebrates. More than a century has passed since the discovery of the first skeleton of Archaeopteryx, but still unknown are the links connecting this momentous find to its reptilian ancestors on the one hand, and to its avian descendants on the other.[16]

Archaeopteryx is a fossilized bird which was discovered in Europe shortly after Darwin published *Origin of Species*. It was enthusiastically declared to be a transition between reptile and bird, because it had small claws on its wings and teeth in its mouth. However, it was a fully formed and functional bird with physical characteristics of a flying bird, including a wishbone and specialized flight feathers. Modern birds do not have teeth, but some ancient birds did, and a few species of birds have wing claws. Archaeopteryx had no imperfectly formed features which would prove it to be transitional between bird and any other kind.

The bird is an extremely distinct class of animal with many differences from reptiles. As we shall learn when we discuss DNA which codifies life, many changes in many parts of its anatomy and physiology would be required to produce a bird from a reptile. A few mutations would not bring this about. A reptile is cold blooded and relies on the sun's rays for its heat, whereas the bird is distinctly warm blooded with the many metabolic processes and controls necessary to produce a warm blooded state. The bird has a quite unique lung which is different from all other animals. It is exceedingly efficient and a principle of the bird lung is one of unidirectional flow of air. There is no diaphragm and the flow of air is not in and out as with other air breathing animals. It is a highly efficient flow-through system with air being continuously delivered through a system of so-called *parabronchi*. The lung is also much larger in birds than in any other animal compared to body size. It not only fills the chest, but also a significant area of the abdominal and bony cavities. The unique respiratory function allows birds to fly at incredible altitudes and to metabolize energy-producing *metabolytes* at astonishing rates. The several unique features of the lungs of birds provide them with the most efficient respiratory system of all animals.[17]

The feather is a highly developed organ which is beautifully constructed for flight and the wing is designed as a remarkable air foil. Feathers for flight are equipped with thousands of barbules which, like velcro, hook together the individual barbs to give great strength with minimal weight. Feathers are not only remarkably constructed for flight but also for insulation. Evolutionists claim feathers "developed" from the scales of reptiles. They make this claim with no rational explanation as to how this remarkable transition occurred and with no fossil evidence of transition. They never attempt to describe the stages of DNA alteration which must have occurred.

Bird bones are light in weight, and although their interior design is what might be termed hollow, there is internal strutting which provides strength. Birds are also equipped with complex navigational systems within their brain which are imperfectly understood despite much scientific study. They navigate by sight, fixation on the stars and sun, magnetic fields, and other unknown mechanisms.

Nature books and biological texts are replete with examples of unique physical, physiological, and instinctive characteristics of various organisms which simply cannot be explained on the basis of Darwinian gradualism, or through chance mutations.

While the fossil record fails to show evidence for the progression of one variety of organism to another, it does clearly demonstrate the stability of types. Evolutionists claim inexorable change by mutation, yet the fossils demonstrate remarkable fixity.

Bees are known to have changed little in what is considered by paleontologists to be 80 million years.

Cockroaches, dragonflies, starfish, bacteria, Ginkgo trees, sharks and many other common organisms of today can be compared to fossils claimed to be 200 to 600 million years old and are essentially unchanged. Thus, rather than portraying progressive change, the fossil record appears to demonstrate remarkable stability of kinds. In a later chapter, "Life," we will see that this is exactly what we would expect because the DNA blueprint is provided with several enzyme systems which correct mistakes in translation.

Austin H. Clark of the U.S. National Museum, who spent many years investigating the relationships of various groups of animals to each other, both fossil and living, affirmed in *The New Evolution Zoogenesis*:

> Since all our evidence shows that the phyla or major groups of animals have maintained precisely the same relation with each other back to the time when the first evidences of life appear, it is much more logical to assume a continuation of these parallel interrelationships further back into the indefinite past, to the time of the first beginnings of life, than it is to assume somewhere in early pre-Cambrian times a change in those interrelationships and a convergence toward a hypothetical common ancestral type from which all were derived. This last assumption has not the slightest evidence to support it.[18]

On page 112, Clark wrote regarding the constancy of kinds:

But we have said enough to show that in the different periods and the different eras the continuous changes affected only the forms within each phylum, and never the interrelationships between the phyla. Most interesting in this connection are the ammonites, for they begin as ammonites, become enormously diversified, and then disappear without ever being anything but ammonites.[19]

In a later chapter Clark said:

. . . the whales and the seals are always whales and seals, and show little or no approach to any other type of mammal. Similarly, there are no intermediates between turtles and snakes, or between turtles and lizards, all of which are reptiles, or between squid and oysters, though both types are mollusks.

. . . No animals are known even from the earliest rocks which cannot be at once assigned to their proper phylum or major group on the basis of the definition of that group as drawn up from a study of living animals alone. A backboned animal is always unmistakably a backboned animal, a starfish is always a starfish, and an insect is always an insect no matter whether we find it as a fossil or catch it alive at the present day.[20]

Although Dr. Clark failed to credit creation to an Almighty God he concluded:

. . . we may assume without the possibility of successful contradiction that all of the major groups of animals were formed at the same time . . . There is no evidence of any kind which would lead us to suppose that any one of the major groups was derived through any of the others.[21]

It would appear Dr. Clark discovered through many

years of patient scientific research what Genesis 1 declares ten times: that God created after their kinds. Paul affirms the same message in 1 Corinthians 15:39, "All flesh is not the same flesh: but there is one kind of flesh of men, another flesh of beasts, another of fishes, and another of birds."

But is it credible to conceive of a being that could create all we know of earth and the universe? Is it credible to believe there is a God so omnipresent and so interested in small details that he could create and maintain such infinite variety as the millions of species that populate the earth?

Yes and no. No, because human intelligence cannot imagine that sort of being. Yes, because God is such a God. He has revealed Himself, from the opening pages of the Bible to its closing, as a God who creates, a God who loves His creation with a love so far superior to ours that we cannot understand. He alone is capable and caring enough to create the incomparable diversity of life witnessed on earth.

Nevertheless, what's clear to many Christians remains obscured by the flotsam of shipwrecked evolution, ever drifting on the surface of our schools and media. This pollution has filtered deep into our basic institutions, our very thought processes. Clearing the waters for our children, for our brothers and sisters in Christ, is no small task. But we must understand the ground that has been lost, and confront the challenge.

[1] Charles Darwin, *The Origin of Species by Means of Natural Selection* (New York: A. L. Burt Co., 1906), pp. 333-334.

[2] A.G. Fisher, "Fossils, Early Life and Atmospheric History," *Proc. Nat. Acad. Sci.*, US53: 1205-15, 1965.

[3] Stephen J. Gould, "Is a New and General Theory of Evolution Emerging?" Paper given at a symposium on evolution, Hobart and William Smith Colleges, Geneva, NY, 1980.

[4] Steven J. Gould, *The Panda's Thumb* (New York, London: W. W. Norton and Co., 1980), p. 181.

[5] G. G. Simpson, *Tempo and Mode in Evolution* (New York, Morningside Heights: Columbia University Press, 1944), p. 106.

[6] T. Storer, *General Zoology* (New York: McGraw-Hill, 1957), p. 216.

[7] E. J. H. Corner, *Contemporary Botanical Thought*, eds. A. M. McLeod & L. S. Cobey (Chicago: Quadrangle, 1961), p. 97.

[8] D. M. Raup and S. M. Stanley, *Principles of Paleontology* (San Francisco: W. M. Greeman and Co., 1971), p. 306.

[9] H. Smith, *From Fish to Philosopher* (New York: Little Brown, 1953), p. 26.

[10] W.E. Swinton, *Biology and Comparative Physiology of Birds*, ed. A. J. Marshall (New York: Academic Press, 1960, Vol. 1), p. 1.

[11] Luther D. Sutherland, *Darwin's Enigma: Fossils and Other Problems* (Santee, CA: Master Book Publishers, 1984).

[12] Ibid., p. 10.

[13] Ibid.

[14] Ibid., p. 88.

[15] Ibid., p. 78.

[16] Donald S. Farmer and James King, eds., *Avian Biology*, Vol. 1 (New York, London: Academic Press, 1971), p. 20.

[17] A. S. King and J. McClelland, *Birds: Their Structure and Function* (London, Philadephia, Toronto, Mexico City, Rio de Janeiro, Sydney, Hong Kong: Balliere Tindall, 1975), pp. 137-142.

[18] Austin H. Clark, *The New Evolution Zoogenesis* (Baltimore: The Williams and Wilkins Co., 1930), p. 104.

[19] Ibid., p. 112.

[20] Ibid., p. 167.

[21] Ibid., p. 212.

# About Mutations and Other Theories

Darwin spent years considering and probably reconsidering his thoughts about how living things came to be what they are. He submitted his thoughts in his first book, *On the Origin of Species by Means of Natural Selection, or the Preservation of Favoured Races in the Struggle for Life,* 28 years after the voyage on the H. M. S. Beagle. He was making his observations and arriving at conclusions with the limited scientific knowledge available to him in the early and mid-nineteenth century.

His genius lay in formulating the conclusion that natural selection is at work in nature, much as occurs in the selection of favored variations by horticulturists and animal breeders. Many of his conclusions are in error because he believed variations of organisms resulted from factors such as learned behavior, use and disuse of organs, a "law of progressive development," etc. Since Darwin, the scientific community has erred in accepting his theories on faith, and not recognizing the difference in his genius and in his errors.

Natural selection is as limited as human selection. We know sugar beets can be selected ad infinitum and their production of sugar reaches a maximum. Thoroughbred horses have been bred for many years, and their speed has been pretty well maximized. Physiology is ruled by the anatomy and enzyme systems of the organism, and these are dependent on the DNA blueprint of each species.

Thus, there is a tremendous difference between "microevolution" which Darwin recognized at Galapagos, and "macroevolution," which he extrapolated from this. This is the major difficulty we have today. God invented and created sources of variation among species, but this variation cannot be exaggerated to presume the creation of new kinds with new organ systems, new protein enzymes, and new concepts. Many leaders in the field of evolution are pretty well agreed that Darwin's original theory cannot be accepted, although they continue to honor him as the person responsible for developing a "rational" system of thought producing the concept of evolution. It is quite reasonable to believe Darwin himself would reject that part of his theory which presumed all kinds evolved from a common ancestor if he had available present day knowledge. Concerning the geological record of fossils he wrote, "Those who believe that the geological record is in any degree perfect will undoubtedly at once reject the theory."[1] He firmly believed the record was imperfect as of his time, and that future generations of paleontologists would be able to find the missing links and cause the record to become perfect. This has not happened. In over 130 years, not one single missing link has been discovered. Not one single example of a family gradually transforming into another family has been found. Billions of fossils have been discovered, and untold amounts of time and money have been spent looking for them. Darwin considered his theory untenable without such links, and so do some critical students of evolution today. In the light of present knowledge it would seem naive to believe or teach Darwin's theory that new families of life evolve by slow, gradual transformation from a common ancestor over vast periods of time.

### Neo-Darwinian Theory

When Darwin developed his theory of evolution the work of Gregor Mendel was not generally recognized, although he published in 1866. He demonstrated that inheritance was governed by separate hereditary units which later became known as genes. When evolutionists heard about genes they developed a so-called *Neo-Darwinian* theory, proposing that mutations supplied the building blocks of change.

Mutations are produced by chance or random alteration in DNA, the genetic code of an organism, and are basically a failure of proper transcription. In other words, they represent misprints, and in general they affect a single gene or group of genes.

Unfortunately for the theory of evolution, there is really no support for the belief that creation can be expected through mutation. J. J. Freidn, in *The Mystery of Heredity*, states,

We have to face one particular fact, one so peculiar that in the opinion of some people it makes nonsense of the whole theory of evolution; although the biological theory calls for incorporation of beneficial variance in the living populations, a vast majority of the mutants observed in any organism are detrimental to welfare. Some are lethal, causing incurable diseases or fetal deaths; others are sub-lethal, killing off or incapacitating most of the carriers or allowing some to escape; still others are sub-vital, damaging health, resistance or vigor in a variety of ways.[1]

C. P. Martin of McGill University writes, in *A Non-Geneticist Looks at Evolution*, "The mass of evidence shows that all or almost all, known mutations are unmistakably pathological and the few remaining ones are highly suspect."[2] H. J. Muller, recipient of the Nobel Prize for his work with mutation, stated, "Most mutations are bad. In fact good ones are so rare that we can consider them all as bad."[3]

It would appear that the Neo-Darwinist has made the same mistake imagining wonderful changes through mutations after learning about DNA that Darwin made before the code of life was understood. Actually, by careful cultivation techniques man has been able to utilize some mutations to benefit agriculture and husbandry. Thus, seedless grapes are a mutation but must be propagated artificially and would never be expected to be a competitor in the wild.

Neo-Darwinists claim evolution is acting even now to

improve species. When pressed for examples they can give very few. The most popular example of evolution by mutation cited by Neo-Darwinists is that of the Peppered Moth (*Biston betularis*) of Great Britain. Before the Industrial Revolution most of these moths were light colored and they blended with the lichen which grew on trees. This camouflage protected them from predator birds. Dark varieties of Peppered Moth were uncommon. During the Industrial Revolution, air pollution resulted in the elimination of lichen on tree bark within some cities, and the dark variety of the moth were noted to increase substantially. The light colored moths continued to predominate in the country, where there was less pollution and lichen continued to offer camouflage.

In 1950, Oxford zoologist Bernard Kettlewell showed through a series of experiments that the birds which feed on these moths are able to find colored moths better on unpolluted lichen covered trees and light colored moths better on polluted trees. Thus he demonstrated the workings of natural selection. However, the dark colored moths were not products of mutations, and the gene for production of pigment was already present within the moth population. The concept of a variation of individuals under these circumstances hardly needs proof. Despite the difference in color, the moths remain moths. With the return of lichen-covered tree trunks after pollution control was effected in Britain, the light colored moths returned to prominence. There was no permanent alteration in genetic availability, and there was no significant change in the character of the moth.

Natural selection was demonstrated, but not evolution of one kind to another.

*Sickle cell anemia* has been claimed as an example of a mutation which has produced a favorable variation. Sickle cell anemia is a serious disease among Blacks, producing severe episodes of pain, fever, and frequently death. It is caused by a mutation in the hemoglobin molecule and results in abnormally shaped red blood cells which are sickle-shaped rather than round. The hemoglobin molecule contains 574 amino acids. The sickle cell trait is produced by a single mistake in the sequence of these amino acids. The amino acid Valine replaces Glutamic acid. This is an illustration of how exact the production of living proteins must be for our bodies to grow and function normally. A single misprint out of 574 sequences results in this serious congenital disease. The symptoms result from clogging of capillaries by the misshapen red blood cells. The sickle cell trait is recessive and the symptomatic disease occurs only in a person who inherits the trait from both parents.

The favorable aspect claimed by Neo-Darwinists consists in the fact that the abnormal hemoglobin is more resistant to malaria than normal hemoglobin. However, sickle cell anemia is itself a very serious congenital disease producing severe bone pain, convulsions, paralysis, and IQ deficiencies in children. Adults suffer similar symptoms, as well as blindness and heart failure with a mortality rate eleven times higher in Jamaicans over age 30 than that experienced by the general population. It produced a maternal mortality of an astounding 33% before modern treatment, and prematurity and fetal death were common. Those of us who have been spared this evolutionary leap can be grateful.

A third example given by Neo-Darwinists involves bacterial resistance to antibiotics. Infecting bacteria are frequently noted to "become" resistant to antibiotics administered to control the infection. Neo-Darwinists are apt to use the term "mutation" to describe this phenomenon, and yet it has nothing to do with mutation. The fact is there are some individuals in cultures of many bacterial varieties which are resistant to some antibiotics. The antibiotic is capable of acting as a selector just as a human breeder would act in animal husbandry. The organisms which are sensitive to the antibiotic are killed off, leaving the resistant ones to flourish. This phenomenon occurs all too frequently and is a well recognized problem in the treatment of many infections with antibiotics. Some would say the bacteria mutated to save the colony. Mutations occur only as chance, accidental transcription errors, and not as a desperate response to the threatened survival of a colony. The suggestion by Neo-Darwinists that it is an example of mutation is simply erroneous. The gene for producing an enzyme to protect bacteria is present within some species, and thankfully not in all. Of interest in this regard is the fact that bacteria isolated from the frozen bodies of two seamen who died during an Arctic expedition in 1848 were found to be resistant to antibiotics developed 120 years later.

Mutations among Drosophila, the fruit fly, have been studied more than any other member of the animal kingdom. It has been subjected to X-radiation, ultraviolet radiation, and various chemical and physical methods known to induce genetic change. Despite changes in wing structure, position of legs, coloration, etc., the specimens continue to be fruit flies.

Theodosius Dobzhansky, world renowned naturalist and an evolutionist, summarized Drosophila mutation experiments as follows:

> The clear-cut mutants of Drosophila melanogaster, with which so much of the classical research in genetics was done, are almost without exception inferior to wild-type flies in viability, fertility, and longevity. Mutation never produced anything new. They had malformed wings, legs and bodies, and other distortions, but they always remained fruit flies. When mutated flies were mated with each other, it was found that after a number of generations, some normal fruit flies began to hatch. If left in their natural state, these normal flies would eventually have been the survivors over the weaker mutants, preserving the fruit fly in the original form.[4]

In a similar vein, G. Ledyard Stebbins disclaimed any positive effects to be expected from mutations. When mutated insects were placed in competition with normal ones the result was always the same. He stated, "After a greater or lesser number of generations the mutants were eliminated."[5] They could not compete because they were not improved, but instead were at a disadvantage.

A succinct judgment of the evolutionary power to be expected from mutation is to be found in the *Encyclopedia Americana*, 1977, Vol. 10, p. 742:

> The fact that most mutations are damaging to the organism seems hard to reconcile with the view that mutation is the source of raw materials for evolution. Indeed, mutants illustrated in biology textbooks are a collection of freaks and monstrosities, and mutation seems to be a destructive rather than a constructive process.

Those who theorize that evolution from simple organisms to complex organisms has resulted from mutations must be unaware of the fact that mutations are practically never helpful. To understand why mutations are generally harmful one should visualize DNA and the chromosomes as being comparable to a computer tape of instruction. A mutation is comparable to allowing a five-year-old child to rewrite a section of highly technical instruction for the production of some machine as complicated as a modern airplane. If the section rewritten were unimportant, the airplane might have USA on the top of the wings instead of on the bottom, and thus not interfere with its capacity to fly. If it involved the design of the engines the plane might well not fly. It is inconceivable that an improvement in the plane could result from scrambled instruction designed by chance. Yet, evolutionists are maintaining that the billions upon billions of improvements in millions of species have occurred by this unlikely mechanism.

The absurdity of all this is hard to believe. The very fact that learned professors and teachers propound these beliefs leads many to believe there must be some merit. The "merit" is fervent faith in the concept of evolution.

The rarity of favorable mutations has been stressed. Considering the millions of varieties of life found on earth it would seem folly to ascribe to chance mutations the ultimate mechanism for the development of the incredibly complex and wonderful forms with the remarkable organs, physiology, and instincts which we find. How does one conceive of the development of an eye with its intricate control mechanism, its ability to transmit light rays into electrical impulses, and its connection with the brain including the ability of the brain to interpret and appreciate the information received? There is no probable evidence that this is the way the myriad forms of life have come to be, and one is compelled to admit this is very shaky ground on which to base such remarkable creation.

On the other hand, variation within kinds is a consistent result of eukariotic (sexual) reproduction. It would appear God ordained variation which would obviously benefit adaptation to changing environment. This so-called micro-evolution has been documented among the birds and insects of Hawaii where subspecies and new species of the same genus are found. This is a far cry from macro-evolution which would necessitate the creation of new organs and concepts. It is not variation itself which is repudiated. It is the power of variation to change one kind into another kind which is denied.

### *Punctuated Equilibrium*

Stephen Jay Gould, Professor of Paleontology at Harvard University, and Niles Eldredge, Curator of Invertebrate Paleontology at the American Museum of Natural History, reject gradualism and advocate a theory of relatively rapid specieation. They maintain that a new species can arise when a small segment of the ancestral population is isolated at the periphery of the ancestral range. Gould has written in *The Panda's Thumb*,

> The history of most fossil species includes two features particularly inconsistent with gradualism: (1) Stasis — Most species exhibit no directional change during their tenure on earth. They appear in the fossil record looking much the same as when they disappear; morphological change is usually limited and directionless. (2) Sudden Appearance — In a local area, a species does not arise gradually by the steady transformation of its ancestors; it appears all at once and 'fully formed.'[6]

He also said of Darwin on page 181,

> The extreme rarity of transitional forms in the fossil record persists as the trade secret of paleontology. The evolutionary trees that adorn our textbooks have data only at tips and nodes of their branches; the rest is inference, however reasonable, not the evidence of fossils. Yet Darwin was so wedded to gradualism that he wagered his entire theory on the denial of this literal record: "the geological record is extremely imperfect and this fact

will to a large extent explain why we do not find inter-
minable varieties, connecting together all the extinct and
existing forms of life by the finest graduated steps. He
who rejects these views on the nature of the geological
record will rightly reject my whole theory."

Darwin's arguments still persist as the favorite escape
of most paleontologists from the embarrassment of a
record that seems to show so little of evolution directly.
In exposing its cultural and methodological roots, I wish
in no way to impugn the potential validity of gradualism (for all general views have similar roots). I wish only
to point out that it was never "seen" in the rocks.

Paleontologists have paid an exorbitant price for
Darwin's argument. We fancy ourselves as the only true
students of life's history, yet to preserve our favored
account of evolution by natural selection we view our
data as so bad that we almost never see the very process
we profess to study.[7]

Punctuated Equilibrium, which is also called Salta-
tion and Macro-evolution, is proposed by Gould and
Eldredge as an answer to the problem of the sudden
appearance of thousands of fully formed creatures in the
Cambrian layer of rocks with little evidence of life in the
Precambrian layer. As indicated, it also recognizes the
continued inability of the fossil record to substantiate
Darwin's theories. Punctuated equilibrium would imply
multiple favorable mutations which we know would be
associated with thousands of unfavorable or even dead-
ly mutations for each favorable one. Such a catastrophic
situation could be imagined only through devastating
exposure to mutagenic factors such as radiation bom-
bardment or extreme ultraviolet radiation. This is the

sort of thing which we fear from atomic warfare and which scientists are joined in warnings of extinction. The results would have been widespread extinction rather than massive creativity.

It would seem that Gould and Eldredge and those who support punctuated equilibrium are actually recognizing creation and calling it by some other name.

This theory has not been accepted by the majority of evolutionists, but their criticism of Darwinian evolution is noteworthy.

### Theistic Evolution

Before beginning my study in depth of the theory of evolution I could have been characterized as a theistic evolutionist. Many Christians probably belong to this school. Theistic evolutionists believe God created life, but having come under the influence of secular education and the world literature, they are led to believe that evolution was God's plan for the creation of the many species which are found extant today or among the fossils. It is in many ways a compromise. It recognizes both God as Creator and evolution as the *modus operandi* of the development of species. In this theory an individual must choose whether man is included in the evolutionary process, or whether he accepts man as a special act of Creation. Quite obviously those who accept the six days of Creation are not tempted in this direction. Those who accept the antiquity of the earth as claimed by geologists may well wonder why God might have spread the creation process out. Some of the calculations geologists use to determine the age of earth are dependent on the theory of evolution itself. I consider age of earth more a problem for geologists than for those of us willing to appreciate God's creative power. I am certain His timing was in His own pleasure and in His own wisdom.

As noted above, I was a theistic evolutionist as a result of being taught evolution as a scientific fact in biology courses in premedical and medical school. My intensive study of evolution in order to relate it to the Genesis account has convinced me evolution as propounded by any theory is without foundation. Unfortunately, many church leaders have readily accepted some version of theistic evolution. Many have unwittingly urged that believers should accept the "scientific" explanation of evolution and withdraw from a confrontation. They have urged that we not "stand" on Genesis or that Genesis does not really mean what it says.

I believe the causes of this dichotomy rest primarily on two difficulties. The first has been suggested in an earlier paragraph. It is hard for an ordinary person who does not carefully study all of the evidence to question the authority of his learned teachers. There is even a certain amount of "logic" to the evidence cited unless one looks at the evidence critically and with basic understanding of biological processes.

The second difficulty is unfortunate. Many of us have shallow faith in the authenticity of Scripture. We are quick to back off from holding fast to the eternal truths which God intends to reveal to us.

To include man as an evolved species is to refute Genesis 1:27 and Genesis 2:7 which declare that God created man in His own image, and that He formed man from the dust of the ground and breathed into his nostrils the breath of life. In general, the ordinary theistic evolutionist is probably quite innocent of any real denial of Scripture. He is taught evolution in secular school and creation in Bible school. The usual Christian probably fails to face seriously the problem of amalgamation of these two views. However, it would seem God considered Genesis of primary importance and this book is written to help the Christian make a decision regarding the authority of the biblical account.

## Extraterrestrial Life

There are two rationales for the belief in extraterrestrial origin of life. Some who believe that life arose on earth by chance postulate that it could well have arisen elsewhere. This idea is championed by Carl Sagan, and great sums of money have been expended funding the search for evidence of extraterrestrial life. Chemical analysis of asteroids and material brought back from the moon has shown no evidence of organic material which might confirm this supposition.

Some who refuse to accept God as Creator and yet recognize that life could not have formed spontaneously on earth find it convenient to believe that life must have come from outer space. The difficulty of explaining how life might have arisen by chance becomes less acute if the problem is transferred into the vast reaches of the universe. There is no evidence of any kind for this theory.

The infinite number of different forms of life is a source of great wonder and confusion to the average human mind. There are over 290,000 species of beetles and at least 675,000 species of insects. The multitudes of varieties of fishes with their special characteristics, instincts, and habitats confuse the mind. It is hard to conceive of God being so omnipresent and so interested in small details that He could create and maintain such infinite variety. And yet, we know that God is such a God. Jesus Christ has assured us that He is interested in each one of us individually, and in every person who has ever lived. The hairs on our head are numbered. He promised Abraham in Genesis 22:17 that his descendants would be numbered as the stars of the heaven, and as the sand which is upon the seashore. This implies that He would know them. If we accept the truth of Scripture we accept the knowledge that God is capable and interested enough to create each individual variety that has so far been catalogued.

I believe evolution has nothing to offer because it is not *Truth*. Its teaching that life could have begun by chance and that we have reached a pinnacle of development through natural selection with man being supreme and with his destiny in his own hands and mind is conspicuously wrong, and opposed to God's position as Creator, Sustainer, and Savior. My personal studies have led me to believe that evolution is false and that society has suffered as a result of this adult fantasy.

The theory of evolution is not a benign sweet process of Nature happily producing new life and better and better circumstances for all. One of its strongest proponents, Sir Julian Huxley, has said, "After Darwin it was no longer necessary to deduce the existence of divine purpose for the facts of biological adaptation."[8] He also said, "In the evolutionary pattern of thought there is no longer need or room for the supernatural. The earth was not created; it evolved. So did all the animals and plants that inhabit it, including our human selves, mind and soul as well as brain and body. So did religion."[9] Another evolutionist has recently claimed that man was not made in the image of God, but rather in the image of an ape. He further claims that God did not make man; but rather that man made God in order to fulfill his own pride.

Actually, for the atheist the origin of matter proposes a greater dilemma than does the origin of life. Most of us never think about the serious questions raised by contemplating the origin of matter and the laws of physics in the absence of a Creator. Most scientists are pretty well agreed that matter is finite, and hence such theories as the "Big Bang" theory and the "Expanding Universe." Some Communist scientists have postulated that matter is eternal and has within it built-in power to create life. A. I. Oparin, Russian biochemist and pioneer researcher on the origin of life, has spent his career in fruitless search for answers to how life began without a Creator. Disregarding the second law of thermodynamics he suggests matter has built-in power to spontaneously and progressively combine into living molecular complexes. Because he hypothesizes matter as eternal he has no problem with its origin, but he fails to explain where all this power comes from.[10]

The materialist suffers from the same delusion as those who believe in the extraterrestrial origin of life. If the process can be moved far enough back in time and far enough away from reality, anything might be possible.

I am unable to accept such fantasy. The hard facts have been accumulating which make spontaneous biogenesis and evolution implausible.

[1]J. J. Friedn, *The Mystery of Heredity* (New York: John Day, 1971), pp. 315-316.
[2]C. P. Martin, "A Non-Genecist Looks at Evolution," *American Scientist*, 41 (1953), 103.
[3]H. J. Muller in *Time, The Weekly Magazine*, 11 November 1946, 96.
[4]Theodosius Dobzhansky, *Heredity and the Nature of Man* (New York: Harcourt, Brace and World, 1964), p. 126.
[5]G. Ledyard Stebbins, *Processes of Organic Evolution* (Englewood Cliffs, NJ: Prentiss-Hall, 1971), pp. 24-25.
[6]Stephen J. Gould, *The Panda's Thumb* (New York, London: W. W. Norton & Company, 1980), p. 182.

[7]Ibid., p. 181.

[8]Julian Huxley, "The Present State of Teleology," *Rationalist Annual*, Transactions of the Victoria Institute (London, 1947), LXXIX 70.

[9]Julian Huxley, "Issues in Evolution," in *Evolution after Darwin* (Chicago: University of Chicago Press, 1960 III), pp. 252f.

[10]Alexander I. Oparin, *The Chemical Origin of Life* (Springfield, IL: Charles C. Thomas, Publisher, 1964), pp. xvi-xvii.

# Life

Life is not easily defined by any terms. It is more easily recognized than scientifically described. It involves and expresses action of one kind or another at the molecular level and at the morphological level. *Reproduction* is an essential characteristic. Reproduction separates life from non-life, for it is not difficult to appreciate the fact that inanimate structures require external forces and intelligence to be produced. We can also recognize that life has an ethereal quality which causes those things which we recognize as being alive to remain functional. When death replaces life, function ceases and decay progresses. By reproduction, living creatures maintain the continuing function and integrity of life.

Life is very complex, and as we have learned more about it we have come to realize with increasing clarity that there is no such thing as "simple" life. True, on a comparative scale there are life forms which are relatively simple as compared to so-called "higher" forms. However, the so-called simple forms must carry out all of the essential functions required to maintain and reproduce life.

## Essentials of Life

There are several absolutely essential physical factors necessary to support life. Those who deny the existence and creative power of God, and who must hypothesize an origin of life by happenstance natural phenomena overlook these several necessities.

First, there is no known life without a cell which is enclosed within a cell membrane. This applies to both plant and animal life. The cell membrane is a complex structure composed of protein and fats. The plant cell membrane which is also composed of protein and fats is surrounded by cellulose which gives the plant rigidity. When viewed through an ordinary microscope after staining techniques the cell membrane appears to be a rather simple envelope. However, the electron microscope has shown its structure to be quite complex with *lipid* (fat) molecules being arranged in two layers and protein molecules interspersed. The cell membrane acts in a semi-permeable manner, allowing some elements to pass through freely, restricting others and actively transporting still others through the membrane. Thus, it protects and nourishes the interior functional elements of the cell and allows waste products and manufactured substances to pass to the exterior. Those elements such as *potassium ions* which are necessary for the proper functioning of the cell are maintained within, and injurious elements are kept out. It allows free diffusion of oxygen into the cell and free diffusion of carbon dioxide out. Certain substances are not physically capable of passing through the membrane by passive, osmotic means. Some of these substances are actively transported by energy driven methods which are poorly understood. The proteins in the cell membrane probably combine with these elements and aid in this transport. Some kidney cells operate by this kind of activity, ridding the body of certain toxins.

*Phagocytosis* occurs at the cell membrane level in many cells. In this process particles which are too large to pass into the cell are engulfed by a small section of the membrane. This section surrounds the particle and then passes into the interior of the cell where it is digested. Energy is obviously required for this active process and to repair the defect left in the cell membrane. Another vital function of the cell membrane is immunological, protecting the cell from invasion by toxins, viruses, and bacteria.

It is axiomatic that life cannot exist in the absence of a cell membrane, and it is equally axiomatic that a cell membrane cannot be brought into being without a living cell. This creates insurmountable difficulty for the evolutionists or for anyone who denies the origin of life by a Creator. There is no way around this difficulty.

Stephen Jay Gould describes in *The Panda's Thumb*[1] an interesting but pathetic historical sequence which relates to this problem. Evolutionists in the late nineteenth century were apparently more enlightened regarding the difficulty of conceiving of spontaneous generation of the machine we call a cell than their more modern counterparts. Ernst Haeckel, who is best known for dishonestly promulgating the discredited theory "ontogeny recapitulates phylogeny," sought to answer this criticism by hypothesizing living substance of unorganized protoplasm which would bridge the gap between the non-living and living state. He named this speculative substance "Monera," which he defined as "an entirely homogeneous and structureless substance, a living particle of albumin, capable of nourishment and reproduction." He wrote, "Every true cell already shows a division into two different parts, i.e., nucleus and plasm. The immediate production of such an object from spontaneous generation is obviously only conceivable with difficulty; but it is much easier to conceive of the production of an entirely homogeneous, organic substance, such as the structureless albumin body of the Monera."[2]

The evolutionists began to search for this "Monera" in earnest. Sir Thomas Henry Huxley, probably Darwin's most enthusiastic and convincing supporter, was one of those who recognized the importance of this "bridge" to the origin of life by natural means, and he led the search. In mud samples obtained ten years previously from the sea bottom near Ireland and preserved in alcohol he discovered a gelatinous substance which exhibited small calcareous plates called *coccoliths* later shown to be fragments of algal skeletons which sink to the bottom after the death of the living algae. Huxley declared this the sought-after "Monera" and named it "Bathybius haeckelii" in honor of Ernst Haeckel.

This "spectacular discovery" was later shown to be nothing more than gelatinous ooze produced by the action of alcohol on ordinary sea mud, a colloidal precipitate of calcium sulfate. There was no life, and no promise. However, before the marvelous evolutionary "discovery" was debunked other evolutionists had found this same kind of material in other parts of the world, and Haeckel speculated that this living film covered the entire ocean floor. Specimens were discovered near Ottawa, Canada, in 1864 and the prominent paleontologist at McGill University, J. William Dawson, was able to define by acute imagination structures resembling canals and it was named *Eozoon canadense*. Darwin himself accepted this "confirmation" of his theory of evolution and, according to Gould, entered Eozoon into the fourth edition of *The Origin of Species*.

Gould explains this scientific fiasco by stating that "all participants in the debate accepted without question the 'obvious' truth that the most primitive life would be homogeneous and formless, diffuse and inchoate." He quotes Huxley as having made the claim that Bathybius "proves the absence of any mysterious power in nuclei, and proves that life is the property of the molecules of living matter, and that organization is the result of life, not life the result of organization."[3] Because this entire scenario has been shown to be false, Huxley's claim is false. The search for life without a cell was thorough and worldwide. It reminds one of the search which has been in progress for many years to find life from outer space, life on other planets, and missing links among the fossils. The search has been futile.

The apostle Paul wrote in Romans 1:21-22, "Because that, when they knew God, they glorified him not as God, neither were thankful; but became vain in their imaginations, and their foolish heart was darkened. Professing themselves to be wise, they became fools." Stephen Jay Gould excuses the unbelievable foolishness of the many evolutionist scientists who were grasping at the untruths of their imaginations as follows:

> Science contains few outright fools. Errors usually have their good reasons once we penetrate their context properly and avoid judgment according to our current perception of 'truth.' They are usually more enlightening than embarrassing — Bathybius was surely inspired error. It served the larger truth of advancing evolutionary theory. — Bathybius inspired a great amount of fruitful scientific work — Orthodoxy can be as stubborn in science as in religion.[4]

The would-be hero of this incredible farce, Sir Thomas Huxley, had this to say: "Irrationally held truths may be more harmful than reasoned errors."[5]

These quotes should remind and warn us that those who do not believe in God are simply not going to accept a Creator. Belief in supernatural creation presupposes God. There is no error too embarrassing, nor any lack of proof in support of alternate theories too convincing to bring them to accept Creation. We can expect a continuing deluge of false doctrine called evolution.

## DNA (Deoxyribonucleic Acid)

Life requires a program, or a blueprint. Scripture says that life was created by the Word. *DNA* might be considered the material expression of the Word. It is the code of life and it is similar in many respects to the magnetic tape of a computer. Each cell of all plants and animals contains a complete copy of the DNA necessary to produce and program the function of the entire organism. It is contained within the cytoplasm or cell matrix of bacteria and blue-green algae (*prokaryotes*) which have no nucleus, and in the nucleus of all other plants or animals, including man.

The structure of DNA was discovered and proclaimed to the world in 1953 by James Watson and Francis Crick, who received the Nobel Prize for their work. It is a complex molecule composed of nitrogen bases, sugar (*deoxyribose*), and a phosphate. The sugar and nitrogen base join together to form what is called a *nucleotide*. These nucleotides are joined in linear fashion by the phosphate into a long chain which represents DNA. The deoxyribose and phosphate form the upright sides of a ladder arrangement, and the nitrogen bases extend across from side to side forming the rungs of a ladder. The ladder is twisted, forming what is described as a double helix or spiral. The twisting turns out to be very important because in its twisted state it is extremely stable, and when it replicates or reproduces itself it begins by untwisting which causes it to unzip where the nuclear bonds hold it together. Appropriate nuclear bases with attached deoxyribose and phosphate then join onto the exposed nuclear bases of each of the resulting single strands of DNA producing two complete new strands with the exact same nucleotide sequences. Several enzyme systems are involved in carrying out this process. Some enzymes are engaged in the process of preventing inaccurate replication, and if a mistake is made these enzymes remove the inaccurate section and replace it with the correct sequences.

There are four different nucleotides which differ by the particular nuclear base of which they are composed. These four bases are *adenine*, *guanine*, *cytosine*, and *thymine*, which are usually abbreviated as A, G, C, and T. The four nucleotides are the alphabet of life, and these "letters" form words of three letters each. With such an alphabet, 64 three-letter combinations are possible. All life on earth is fabricated, operated, and reproduced by this alphabet which produces a specific code for every individual life form, be it plant or animal. It is therefore a concept, and it is clear all life was engineered with and by this principle. Links of DNA make up the genes, and groups of genes compose the chromosomes.

Like our own language DNA is a symbolic language. Each cell contains a complete copy of the DNA which is the blueprint for that particular organism. Special genes and enzymes encode the program necessary for that particular cell. The number of words encoded for the simple bacterium E. coli is estimated to be three million, which would fill three volumes of 1,000 pages with 1,000 words per page. Human DNA is estimated to represent three billion words which would fill 3,000 volumes of 1,000 pages with 1,000 words per page. The human DNA strand is folded within the nucleus of each of our cells and if opened out would produce a strand three inches in length. This represents the ultimate in miniaturization.

The function of DNA is difficult for our minds to comprehend. During embryological development it must replicate a strand of DNA for each cell of the body which is to be formed. The human body is composed of about 1,000 different kinds of cells, and there are estimated to be about $10^{14}$ (100 trillion) cells in the average human. The structural and enzymatic proteins must be synthesized for each cell. The special sense organs in the nervous system connections must be constructed. About 10 billion nerve cells are needed in the brain for memory and problem solving.

### RNA (Ribonucleic Acid)

RNA is a functional, partial copy of DNA with the task of producing proteins. Whereas DNA is a double strand and resides in the nucleus of a cell, RNA is a single strand which is formed by what is known as transcription from DNA, and exists in the cytoplasm (extranuclear material of the cell where it does its work).

Actually, several components of RNA are formed and participate in an extraordinarily complex system of protein synthesis. The master RNA molecule is a copy of a particular gene, and other forms of RNA act, of all things, to choose and deliver amino acids in proper sequence to the protein strand being produced. Another form of RNA produces a little protein factory called a *ribosome*.

Life is not possible without this complicated arrangement for the production of proteins. To conceive of this coming into being without super intelligence requires mind-boggling faith in chance.

What we call genes are really sections of DNA which produce special strands of RNA whose function it is to code for the thousands of different proteins. Each cell in the body is under the direction of its own set of genes to produce the proteins it needs for its particular function. Control devices similar to thermostats and rheostats were invented long before men conceived of the idea. Does all this seem possible to you by chance alone? People who do not believe in God really have no alternative. Does this mean we have to give credence to their wild conjectures, agree it is science, and apologize for God's claim in Genesis?

In DNA and RNA we may see another realm of understanding of God's promise that man will be made in His image. DNA can be reckoned to be the word of life. Just as Jesus is the Word made flesh (John 1:1), DNA is the word made flesh. As the Holy Spirit moves and demonstrates God's power, so RNA is the action portion of the trinity of life. The ethereal qualities of life which we cannot truly understand are symbolic of God the Father. As God the Father is spirit, which none have seen, there is no understanding the ethereal qualities of life.

Evolutionists err in seeing descent from a common progenitor in all this. This is another example of the truth being usurped. Believers may understand that God conceived of one way that all life would be established. The concept is single. The plant is different from the animal only because its DNA and RNA produce different proteins to build different bodies to do the work they are created to perform.

I am sure "in His image" means more than this, because it was said of man, and we know man is truly different. We know by faith and experience he has a spirit which can commune with God. However, I believe that it is significant that all of life is patterned like the Life described in Scripture. DNA, like Jesus, brings order, purpose, beauty, direction, and life to God's other creations. DNA, also like Jesus, produces life from light.

### Life is a Machine

As indicated previously, life requires a cell and the cell body is an extremely complex machine. It is a tiny factory doing many complicated and interesting things. It contains several so-called *organelles* which have separate enclosing membranes made of *lipids* (fats) and proteins. These organelles are small factories themselves.

## Ribosomes

*Ribosomes* are organelles within the cell body which are vital to the mechanism of protein synthesis. They are found in all living cells. Being extremely small, their structure was not appreciated until electron microscopy was developed. They are barely visible in the ordinary laboratory light microscope, but their three-dimensional configuration has been determined by electron micrographs. A typical bacterial cell contains about 10,000 of them, and the cell of higher animals contains many times more. In general, the more active the cell the more ribosomes it contains.

Ribosomes are composed chiefly of RNA and specific functions of protein production occur at various sites within this extraordinary little machine.

## Proteins

*Proteins* comprise ten to twenty percent of the mass of cells. Structural proteins act as building blocks of cell structures including cell membrane, nuclear membranes, and various organelles. These proteins tend to be arranged in long chains producing minute fibers. Other proteins are enzymes which interact with various chemical or molecular elements within the cell or within organ systems. They do the work of the cell. Their architecture tends to be globular in shape with special reactor areas exposed to the watery medium of the cell so that reactions can take place. Other proteins called *globulins* are involved in immunity and circulate within the blood vessels. Still other proteins are conjugated with special substances for special purposes. *Nucleoproteins* are combinations of proteins with nucleic acid found in DNA and RNA. *Mucoproteins* are combinations of proteins with polysaccharides and are important in digestion. There are several others which perform essential functions in the body. It would seem to require a very fertile imagination to conceive of living proteins coming into existence by pure chance before there was a living cell. No one has been able to guess at a possible acceptable method by which this might have occurred. A living cell containing a blueprint of DNA and the various forms of RNA operating within a ribosome factory are essential for their production.

Amino acids which make up proteins are complex organic compounds which have spatial configurations. The biochemical formula for an amino acid is traditionally written in a two-dimension formula such as:

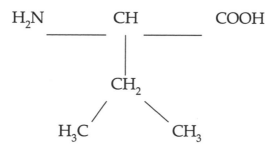

However, they actually exist in a three-dimensional pattern, and the three-dimensional shape can differ, just as your right and left hands differ. Thus, when produced in a laboratory all except *glycine* are 50 percent right-handed (*dextro*) and 50 percent left-handed (*levo*) in configuration. The dextro and levo forms contain the same atoms, but they are as different as your two hands, being mirror images. Now pay attention and get this: living proteins are composed of 100 percent levo forms! The cell is able to accomplish this selection rapidly and with 100 percent accuracy, but sophisticated methods and considerable energy are required for scientists to accomplish this in the laboratory. On top of that, whenever separation into pure forms is accomplished in the laboratory they quickly revert to 50 percent mixtures of D and L forms. Does this give you pause regarding the chance for spontaneous origin of life? Ask your learned professor to explain this hitch. Actually, evolutionists avoid this issue, and do not have any reasonable explanation for this miraculous circumstance. Equally significant, and equally baffling, is the fact that the sugars of all living carbohydrates are dextro in configuration!

## *Nucleus*

All cells except bacteria and blue-green algae contain a *nucleus* which is enclosed in a nuclear membrane composed of lipid and protein. The nucleus controls the metabolic and productive functions of the cell. It contains the DNA which represents the many genes of the organism. These genes are arranged end-on-end and determine the protein enzymes, structures, and chemicals which are produced by the cells of the organism.

During reproduction of the cell the DNA within the nucleus is reproduced, forming two exact duplicates. After duplication of DNA, mitosis or cell division follows and each of the two cells resulting contain a nucleus with a complete copy of the DNA.

## *Centrioles*

*Centrioles* play an important role during cell division. Two pairs of centrioles lie near the nucleus. Each centriole is a cylindrical body which contains nine small microtubules. The centrioles of each pair are arranged at right angles to each other. During cell division the two pairs move apart and form a spindle made of microtubules. This arrangement becomes the mitotic apparatus upon which the two sets of chromosomes are separated. Two daughter nuclei and the cell bodies are formed.

## *Mitochondria*

*Mitochondria* are present within all eukaryotic cells, and because they are responsible for energy conversion they are more numerous in cells involved in high energy utilization. They are considered the "power houses" of cells. They produce a substance called *adenosine triphosphate* (ATP) from nutrients supplied to the cell. Adenosine triphosphate is a high energy molecule which the cell uses for most of its energy requirements.

The production of this source of energy within the mitochondria involves a series of extremely complex chemical reactions which are facilitated by the enzymes within the mitochondria. The energy is required in three primary categories of cellular function: (1) transport of substances through membranes; (2) synthesis of various biochemical substances such as cholesterol, proteins, etc.; (3) mechanical work such as muscle contraction.

Some protein molecules contain several thousand amino acids. During the production of these proteins each *peptide linkage* between these amino acids requires the energy of three ATP molecules. It is therefore apparent that protein synthesis requires much ATP.

### Cilia and Flagella

Some cells in the respiratory tract and fallopian tubes contain *cilia* which are covered by cell membrane and project from the cell like minute hairs. A cilium contains nine microtubules arranged around the periphery of the cilium and two are located in the center. Cilia move in rhythmic fashion and effectively move mucus along the surface. The exact mechanism of their action is incompletely understood, but ATP supplies the energy.

*Flagella* are similar to cilia but are single and supply motion to the cell. Sperm move by the power of a flagellum. The forward mobility of the sperm is produced by a rotary motion of the flagellum which is powered by an incredible little motor at the base of the flagellum. Some would say this little motor built itself by pure chance. I am personally not aware of any little motor which built itself.

### Endoplasmic Reticulum

The *endoplasmic reticulum* is a system of tubules producing a network which extends throughout the cell. It is probably a transport system designed to carry nutrients and manufactured products to various parts of the cell and to the exterior. The membrane composing the endoplasmic reticulum is made of protein and lipid similar to the cell membrane.

### Golgi Complex

*Golgi complexes* are connected with the endoplasmic reticulum and are more numerous in secretory cells. They are believed to store and perhaps refine special secretory products of the cell. They may synthesize carbohydrates and combine them with proteins to form glycoproteins which are constituents of mucus, cartilage, and bone.

### Lysosomes

*Lysosome* organelles are enclosed within a membrane and contain digestive enzymes. They actually represent an intracellular digestive system. Organic compounds which enter the cell are digested into simpler amino acids, glucose, etc. It is the lysosome's function to digest and remove undesirable substances such as dead bacteria, viruses, and the worn-out components of the cell.

### Microtubules

These are very thin tubular structures which are usually arranged in bundles and appear to offer rigidity to other cellular parts such as cilia and flagella. They have recently been shown to serve as conduits for fluid movement within the cell.

### Secretory Granules

Cells store enzymes, hormones, and other secretory products in *secretory granules* within the cytoplasm. This stored material is available for release when the cell receives a message of need. Obviously, enzymes must be present to release the stored secretion.

### Chloroplasts

Plant cells are similar in many respects to animal cells. However, in addition to the cell membrane an outer cell wall composed of cellulose furnishes a certain amount of rigidity to plants necessary for their upright growth.

Plant cells contain *chloroplasts* within which photosynthesis occurs by the action of chlorophyll. By photosynthesis the energy of sunlight is converted into the chemical energy of glucose. As discussed earlier, glucose becomes converted into the high energy compound ATP within the mitochondria of plant and animal cells. The glucose is produced from carbon dioxide and water utilizing the energy of light, and oxygen is a byproduct of the reaction. Thus, through photosynthesis, an extremely complex process, and the production of ATP from the glucose produced, light becomes the driving force of life. Spiritual and physical life share the concept of the interaction of light and life.

Psalm 36:9 — "For with thee is the fountain of life: in thy light we shall see light."

Psalm 27:1 — "The Lord is my light . . . . the Lord is the strength of my life."

John 1:4 —"In him was life; and the life was the light of men."

John 6:33 —"For the bread of God is he which cometh down from heaven, and giveth life unto the world."

John 8:12 — " . . . I am the light of the world: he that followeth me shall not walk in darkness, but shall have the light of life."

Again the sequence of creative events in Genesis is shown to be proper, for we are told that light was established on day one (Genesis 1:3), preceding plant life on day three (Genesis 1:11), preceding animal life on day five (Genesis 1:20).

The invention of chlorophyll and photosynthesis rivals the miracle of the invention of life, and must be recognized as a requirement for both plant and animal life. Those who maintain the implausible possibility of the chance origin of life must add to it the implausible possibility of the simultaneous invention of photosynthesis! How far can imagination be carried?

Photosynthesis is an extremely complicated process which requires special genes (composed of nucleoproteins within the DNA of the plant or bacterial cell), chloroplasts made of lipids and proteins which are made of 100 percent levo amino acids under the direction of the genes, and special chemical agents such as quinone, pheophytin, cytochrome, etc. The process is still poorly understood, but photosynthesis essentially transfers energy from photons of light into carbohydrates.

Machines do not make themselves. A machine is a contrivance which is produced by design (intelligent thought), and for a purpose. Extensive discussion would seem to be unnecessary to establish this truth. Persons may search their own experience to realize a machine has never been observed which came into existence by chance or by accident. An explosion does not produce functioning machines. An explosion can change the shape or configuration of matter, but it cannot rearrange matter into a machine which has a purpose and a function.

Man has attempted without success to create machines with the help of sophisticated computers which would reproduce themselves. Machines are all designed by intellect and individually made by extrinsic work.

Darwin lived at a time when he was not privileged to the information contained in this chapter. He could not have known how intricate the mechanisms and chemical reactions of life are. As a matter of fact, we are still ignorant of a complete understanding of how any of the organelles which have been described operate. Our knowledge of regulatory mechanisms, messenger units, initiator and stop functions, etc., is quite incomplete.

In all this it would appear foolish to ascribe to pure chance and to accidental mutations the power of having accomplished all this. Before anyone teaches or accepts this possibility he should have clear facts with chemical equations and fossil evidence to support it. Atheists have an obvious bias. Unfortunately, our western academic scientists are under serious restraints, because it is difficult to publish anything but evolutionary theory in the usual academic and scientific press. It must also be recognized that advancement in professional circles is fairly contingent on proclaiming the evolutionary doctrine. The many who are not so constrained should look at these facts with great care, giving God the glory, enjoying His creation, and accepting His Word as truth.

[1]Stephen J. Gould, *The Panda's Thumb* (New York, London: W. W. Norton & Company, 1980), pp. 236-244.
[2]Ibid., p. 237.
[3]Ibid., p. 240.
[4]Ibid., p. 243.
[5]Ibid., p. 244.

# Bet Against God?

Open a can of beans, and what do you expect? Beans. No little bugs. No invisible bacteria that will give you food poisoning. If the food was properly sterilized and the container was not breached, you can eat your beans without worrying that some strange organisms are sneaking into your stomach.

Preserving food in this way is more than a modern convenience. It rests on modern science. Until Louis Pasteur in the last century, there was no such understanding about the origins of little worms and flies that seemed to suddenly appear around decaying food or animals. Common knowledge was that life could spontaneously generate.

This piece of folklore was most convenient when Darwinism burst on the scene. If life could basically create itself, this removed a major hurdle in the long, long path called evolution. However, Darwin's successors were to find out it was far more difficult than ever imagined to explain how inert molecules suddenly took on life. But, like Darwin, they were quite willing to speculate and theorize to degrees of absurdity to prove the unprovable.

## *From Whence Fruit Flies?*

From ancient times, common observations appeared to confirm spontaneous generation of life: maggots infested dead animals; mold grew on stale bread; fruit flies were produced on rotting fruit. Some curious scientists attempted experiments to prove or disprove spontaneous generation, but the results were contradictory, presumably because of faulty methodology.

In 1668, Italian biologist Francesco Redi proved that if flies were kept from laying eggs in decaying meat, no maggots would materialize. Then in the nineteenth century, scientists discovered bacteria and other microorganisms, raising anew the possibility of spontaneous generation. Pasteur took on this challenge by heating a fluid enough to destroy all microbes and keeping it sealed. Sure enough, no living organisms were reintroduced. This same basic process — *pasteurization* — is used to preserve food and milk today.

In an 1864 lecture, Pasteur told how in his experiment he sterilized his drop of water full of microscopic organisms.

> I wait, I watch, I question it — begging it to recompense for me the beautiful spectacle of the first creation. But it is dumb, dumb ever since these experiments were begun several years ago; it is dumb because I have kept it from the only thing that man does not know how to produce: from the germs which float in the air, from Life, for Life is a germ and a germ is life. Never will the doctrine of

spontaneous generation recover from the mortal blow of this simple experiment.[1]

Pasteur settled the matter for good, at least for most scientists: life arises only from pre-existing life. This is known as the *law of biogenesis*, and has been proved over and over. Yet, evolutionists claim it did happen, once upon a time!

### Test Tube Creation

Enter *abiogenesis*. Committed evolutionists, wanting to evict God from even the earliest stages of creation, desperately want to believe life arose from inanimate matter. By going back far enough in time, and perhaps far enough from reality, they purport to have found an environment where the god of Chance could zap life into non-living matter.

The obvious challenge to evolutionists was to replicate some kind of spontaneous generation from a concoction of imagined primordial soup. Stanley Miller gave it a shot in 1953.

First he composed an "atmosphere" of hydrogen, methane, ammonia, and water. This combination was chosen not because there is good reason to believe this reflected the atmosphere of a young earth, but because it was thought organic compounds could result from such a menu. In other words, he stacked the deck to begin with, just in case Chance was a less than omnipotent god.

Furthermore, Miller's omission of oxygen is suspect. Much evidence indicates oxygen was present at earth's beginning. Yet oxygen would have destroyed any spontaneously formed amino acid, which is a building block of life. And if there was no oxygen, there would have been no ozone shield in the atmosphere, such as we have today, to absorb lethal quantities of ultraviolet radiation that would otherwise destroy life.

But let's suspend these formidable problems and trace Miller's experiment. Exposing his gases to an electric spark — what evolutionists say may have been lightning — several amino acids were produced. Proteins, which are necessary for life, require twenty "essential" amino acids. Also, the amino acids were not compatible for life. One half were D-forms and one half were L-forms. Living proteins require all L-forms. In spite of these unsolved difficulties, the experiments of Miller have encouraged evolutionists to believe the building blocks of life could have built themselves.

### Beating the Odds

Let's project the Miller experiment further to see what kind of probabilities exist for complete formation of life. The basic unit of life is a cell. The cell includes proteins, which together consist of hundreds, even thousands of amino acids. *All* must be L-forms and *they must be in an exact sequence.*

The simplest living organism known is the very small, bacteria-like *Mycoplasma hominis* H39. It has about 500 different kinds of protein molecules, each of these composed of an average of 400 amino acids. Remember, each protein must have its amino acids in an exact sequence to function.

To get some idea of sequence probabilities, consider that there is only one chance in 17,000 to draw the sequence A-B-C from a pile of 26 letters. How about drawing the nine-letter word "evolution?" One chance in five trillion!

But start calculating the probability of spontaneous generation, and you leave behind the familiar language of thousands, millions, and trillions. Enter, instead, a mathematical twilight zone where probability is so remote that only inverse powers of ten — one divided by numbers with hundreds, even thousands of zeros — can adequately express the odds.

Those kinds of odds represent the chance of having the required pool of only L-form amino acids available for this miraculous combination. Imagine a solution with one billion amino acids, half L-form and half D-form. Now, envision separating half of those acids, at random, and coming out with nothing but L-forms. Statisticians have another name for such astronomical odds: impossibility.

But even if this ideal pool of L-forms somehow segregated itself, what is the probability of obtaining the correct order of amino acids for the formation of just one of the protein molecules in Mycoplasma hominis? One in $10^{520}$ (1 followed by 520 zeros).

Still fishing for the slightest glimmer of hope for spontaneous generation? Don't put your baited hooks into the primordial pond yet. Mycoplasma hominis requires at least 500 different proteins. This would raise the odds of its formation to even more absurd levels, far more than 500 times $10^{520}$.

### *"You are Mistaken"*

Cell development in this primitive environment "poses Herculean problems," wrote French molecular biologist Jacques Monod. He says the "origin of the genetic code [DNA] . . . is not so much a problem as a veritable enigma."[2] Francis Crick, who won the Nobel Prize for his discovery of DNA in 1953, wrote that even with all modern knowledge at his fingertips, man could only conclude that "the origin of life appears at the moment to be almost a miracle, so many are the conditions which would have had to have been satisfied to get it going."[3]

Those who take Genesis as God's revelation of Creation, of course, have no quarrel with miracles. The real mental difficulty is seeking divine answers through human wisdom. Jesus commented on similar vanity when a group of Sadduccees tried to trick Him with a question about which husband a woman of multiple marriages would be united with in heaven: "Ye do err, not knowing the scriptures, nor the power of God" (Matt. 22:29).

What numbers and common sense tell us cannot happen can indeed be accomplished through the power of God. Man, failing to understand Scripture, will reach mistaken conclusions about God's power. Evolutionists are left to their own cleverness. Such inventiveness more often takes the form of desperation, as seen in the frantic search for "Monera" in the last chapter, which produced only mud.

[1]R. Valery-Radot, *The Life of Pasteur* (New York: Dover Publications, 1960), p. 109.

[2]J. Monod, *Chance and Necessity* (London: Collins, 1972), p. 135.

[3]Francis Crick, *Life Itself* (New York: Simon and Schuster, 1981), p. 88.

# Special Gifts

As a general and thoracic surgeon, I have a unique opportunity to observe the human body in action. Because scientific knowledge has progressed to its present state, the functions of a living organism can be understood to be surpassingly ingenious. Yet, we are merely at the periphery of knowledge of molecular biology.

There was a time when so little was known about biological structure and function that it was easy to consider observed phenomena with a considerable amount of naive acceptance. Scientists have now accumulated sufficient knowledge about many biological phenomena to cause us to realize that almost any physical or physiologic aspect of biology has to be considered with awe.

Charles Darwin, whose theories were expressed in *The Origin of Species* in 1859, suffered serious spiritual problems caused by his basic ignorance of biology, although he was considered ahead of his time and is today revered by many as the author of the theory of evolution. He based his theory on the principle that the wonders of biology were developed through the action of pain and suffering and death.[1] He believed universal pain and suffering were incompatible with the biblical teachings that God was loving and compassionate and at the same time almighty.

Darwin was in the same boat with the Sadducees whom Jesus accused of not knowing Scripture (Matt. 22:23-29). Darwin did not appreciate that suffering and death came into God's creation through man's sin, nor that God had already provided for the relief of pain and suffering by several biological mechanisms which we know about now.

As we briefly discussed in Chapter 5, when we see a cheetah chase down and kill a Thompson gazelle on a television nature film, we assume the gazelle feels pain. We now know that much of the pain related to violence is prevented by opiates produced in our bodies. We know humans frequently feel no immediate pain when they are injured. Nine opiate type substances have been identified in various locations of the brain and spinal cord which act on what is referred to as the "analgesia system." The more important of these agents are:

> B-endorphin
> met-enkephalin
> leu-enkephalin
> dynorphin

These substances are released during periods of acute stress. Animals have a generous supply, and it would be difficult to rationalize the existence of these opiate substances on a purely chance, evolutionary basis. These opiates act on the same brain centers in the same way opiates such as morphine and codeine act. I view it as a gift of a compassionate God who also gave us the promise of a Redeemer in Genesis 3:15 when he declared to the serpent, "I will put enmity between thee and the woman, and between thy seed and her seed; it shall bruise thy head, and thou shalt bruise his heel."

Our bodies are constantly vigilant to protect us from harmful outside agents. When I perform an elective operation on a person, their body recognizes my knife as a dangerous attacker, and the pre-supplied mechanisms spring into action to restore the sanctity and *homeostasis* which existed before the knife did its "damage." Endorphins and enkephalins are produced to help relieve pain. Blood clotting is enhanced to reduce blood loss, blood volume is supported by a shift of tissue fluid into the blood vessels; and blood flow is shifted to better guarantee adequate flow to vital organs. To help defend against infection the white blood cells are mobilized by factors which are not yet understood and directed to congregate at the site of tissue injury. The T-cells which we have come to appreciate recently because they are the targets of the AIDS virus play a prominent role in this. "Inflammatory cells" engulf and kill bacteria and digest the dead tissue cells. Healing occurs by the ingrowth of blood vessels and the proliferation of cells called *fibroblasts* which produce scaffolding and scar tissue.

Meanwhile, other changes occur throughout the body to participate in the healing process. The body temperature tends to elevate and many metabolic processes are activated. The heart rate and cardiac output is increased, muscle cells are reduced to supply amino acids for wound healing and glucose is released from stores in the liver and muscles.

These processes are less vigorous and prolonged when the injury or operation is minor and when the animal or person is in good condition. They are initiated and directed by many hormones and enzyme systems produced by various organs and glands such as the brain, pituitary gland, hypothalamus, adrenal glands, etc. We have extensive knowledge of some of these, but we know little or nothing about many.

Dr. Paul Brand,[2] master surgeon and medical missionary to India where he worked among the lepers, has pointed out in a personal communication how important the appreciation of pain is to our bodies. The appreciation of pain gives us the freedom to perform routine acts such as walking, cooking, and handling rough objects, without the necessity of consciously avoiding injury to our skin. The leprosy germ attacks the nerve pain fibers, and a rock in a shoe can produce a painless, crippling ulcer. The same deficiency occurs in some diabetics, and results in disabling and even life-threatening injuries which may be painless.

Unbeknown to Darwin and to many of us, God has given us pain for protection, as well as protection from pain itself. Dr. Brand also teaches that pain is increased by four states and decreased by four opposites. Fear and anger increase and peace and forgiveness decrease; idleness and loneliness increase and action and visitation decrease. The spiritual teachings of Jesus affect our bodies as well as our spirits. I find it impossible to believe that these processes were developed by pure chance, guided by pain, suffering and death. This is what evolution teaches. Are you willing to accept evolutionist claims that these remarkable hormones and biochemical agents came into existence by pure chance? Does it make any sense to you that processes which require a whole chapter in a medical textbook to describe could have developed themselves by haphazard, undirected, senseless, purposeless, accidental transcription errors in the DNA code of life?

[1]Sir Gavin de Beer, *Charles Darwin* (Garden City, New York: Doubleday and Company, Inc., 1964), p. 266.
[2]Dr. Paul Brand, personal communication, October, 1982.

# Searching for Uncle Ape

Genesis 1:26, "And God said, Let us make man in our image, after our likeness: and let them have dominion over the fish of the sea, and over the fowl of the air, and over the cattle, and over the earth, and over every creeping thing that creepeth upon the earth."

This prophesy was and is being fulfilled. The Genesis account tells it all. Man is, indeed, master of everything that creepeth upon the earth. We have no enemies which are truly threatening except ourselves. If one thinks about it, this would make no sense from an evolutionary viewpoint. The instincts of the creatures of the earth are not programmed to cause direct harm to man, and so there is an obvious limit put upon them regarding their relationship to man. Man is not a food source for any animal. In general, animals fear man.

No other animals enjoy such natural protection. Even elephants fear man, and we know their ultimate fate is in man's hand at this very time.

Popular evolutionist dogma now proposes that man descended from apes. Darwin initially avoided suggesting this possibility to avoid producing what he termed "prejudice against" his theory of natural selection. However, when he published *The Descent of Man* in 1870, he made clear his opinion that man was, like all other species, descended from a common progenitor. Alfred Wallace, who independently developed a theory of natural selection similar to that of Darwin, disagreed about the evolution of man, believing the human brain could not have developed through this means. Wallace maintained that man was a special creation.

In *The Descent of Man*, Darwin cited no fossil or other concrete evidence to support his belief. There are many varieties of primates today which include lemurs, monkeys, chimpanzees, orangutans, gorillas, and gibbons. If there was descent of any primates to man one might ask why there are no "inferior" specimens partially evolved today in some primitive enclave. Actually, the theory of evolution is responsible for the assumption by many in the nineteenth century that some races were, indeed, inferior.

The evolution of man from apes has been a very popular proposition with evolutionists, and especially with the press. A single tooth which may be claimed to be humanoid sends cartoonists rushing to the drawing boards to construct pictures of possible "ape-men," replete with hair and all.

The search for "missing links" has continued since Darwin's time. Despite 130 years of searching there are no fossils that have convincingly related man to any other species. Most have been conclusively proven false, and at least one was a decided fraud. It is disappointing that these false claims have been greeted with enthusiasm by many authorities of natural history. Several have been presented for many years as "proofs" of man's evolution only to be recanted ignominiously.

## Neanderthal Man

The first fossil claimed to be intermediate was the so-called *Neanderthal Man*, found in the Neander Valley near Düsseldorf, Germany, in 1856. Darwin heard of this finding, but apparently made no effort to view it. Instead, his close friend Thomas Huxley carefully studied the skull fragment and some long bones. The skull was thick, with large ridges over the eyes. It had already been declared by the great pathologist Rudolf Virchow as an old man with gout.

Huxley found its skull capacity and hence its brain equal to that of modern man. Its limb bones were considered by Huxley to be those of a European of middle stature. He considered him allied to the higher apes, but definitely a man. Neanderthal Man was immediately pictured as being bent, stupid looking, hairy, and ape-like — the prototype of ape-men ever since. Many Neanderthal skeletons have been found since then, and we know the original specimen was badly deformed by disease. Men of similar character and ancestry have been found in France and are called *Cro-Magnon*. Neanderthal and Cro-Magnon men are now recognized as being fully human, with a skull capacity slightly larger than modern man. He was fully erect, and cave paintings and artifacts show he was sophisticated, intelligent, and sensitive. Because many lived in the caves of Europe they have been called "cave men."

## *Java Man*

Eugene Dubois, a Dutch physician, determined that he would be the person to discover the "missing link." He accepted an appointment as a surgeon with the Royal Dutch Army in 1887 in Sumatra, where he reasoned man's ancestors might be found. Sure enough, he discovered a skull cap, three molar teeth, and a thigh bone on the Island of Java in 1891. He named his specimen *Pithecanthropus erectus* and announced to the world he had found the missing link. There followed much controversy, but finally many evolutionists accepted Pithecanthropus erectus as man-like. Later Dubois admitted finding true human skulls in the same rock formations in which the bones of his specimen were found. Still later he changed his opinion about Pithecanthropus erectus and considered the skull cap that of an ape or gibbon. Expeditions to the same area later found only skull fragments and teeth of chimpanzees and gibbons. Despite all this, *Java Man* or *Homo erectus* is still referred to in some textbooks and professional literature as an example of man's evolution from apes.

A problem in determining the significance of the finding of ape-like skeletons with human bones and artifacts is the fact that apes of all types have been favorite foods of many primitive peoples. The brains of apes are relished, and the skulls are broken to gain access. *Peking Man* may well have been an instance of this confusion. Peking Man has been proclaimed an example of a link between apes and humans, but the story of Peking Man is as unsatisfactory as that of Java Man. There are several unsatisfactory circumstances surrounding the claim, and one of the most unusual is that the bones disappeared. There are several stories about this disappearance, but none are verifiable. It seems probable Peking Man was a mixture of the bones of humans who lived in a cave and the bones of the apes which they ate.

## Piltdown Man

*Piltdown Man* was announced to the world with much fanfare in 1912 and given the scientific name *Eoanthropus dawsoni*. He was discovered in a gravel pit near Piltdown, England, by Charles Dawson, a lawyer and amateur paleontologist. The skull fragments were human in shape and the jaw was ape-like, with two molar teeth which showed the type of wear typical of human teeth and never seen in apes. Piltdown Man was acclaimed by the world's greatest authorities as an ape-man who had lived 500,000 years before. He was proclaimed to be a missing link in textbooks and professional literature for over forty years.

In 1949, Kenneth P. Oakley applied a fluorine test which he had developed to the Piltdown specimens and found they contained very little fluorine. Bones absorb fluorine from soil in which they lie, and the amount they pick up is a function of time. It was apparent that these bones had not been long in the gravel pit.[1] Oakley, J. S. Weiner, and W. E. leGros Clark later determined the skull and jaw had been specially stained, and the teeth filed to appear human. It was quite apparent when Piltdown was finally submitted to scientific study that it was a hoax. The skull was indeed completely human, and the jaw was that of a modern orangutan.

The author or authors of this travesty remain unknown to this day. It should be a far greater embarrassment to evolutionists than it is. In *The Panda's Thumb*, Stephen Jay Gould, writing about "Piltdown Revisited" said, "All this speculation provides endless fun and controversy . . . "[2] He later comments, "If we are to learn anything about the nature of scientific inquiry from Piltdown — rather than just reveling in the joys of gossip —."[3] These statements fail to express the sincere regret due to the lay public for the unscholarly acceptance of this specimen by the scientific community. Gould does ask the appropriate question, "Why had anyone believed Piltdown in the first place? It was an improbable creature from the start."[4]

Mr. Gould points out that there were many detractors. C. W. Lyne, who was a dental anatomist, had warned early on that a canine tooth found in the same

gravel pit had been artificially worn down. Other warnings were issued. David Waterston of King's College,
University of London, stated, according to Gould, "It
seems to me to be as inconsequent to refer the mandible
and the cranium to the same individual as it would be to
articulate a chimpanzee foot with the bones of an essentially human thigh and leg." Gould adds, "The correct
explanation had been available from the start, but hope,
desire, and prejudice prevented its acceptance."[5]

Mr. Gould, who teaches geology, biology, and the history of science at Harvard University, points out, . . . "the
three leading lights of British anthropology and paleontology — Arthur Smith Woodward, Grafton Elliot Smith,
and Arthur Keith — had staked their careers on the reality of Piltdown. (Indeed, they ended up as two Sir Arthurs
and one Sir Grafton, largely for their part in putting
England on the anthropological map.)"[6] These three paleontologists were thus knighted for innocently abetting a
terrible hoax on the scientific world and on those seeking
truth. Furthermore, he shows no regret in reporting that
if Pierre Teilhard de Chardin, whom he claims to be an
accomplice of Dawson's fraud, had confessed in 1918 that
his "promising career" would have ended. Teilhard de
Chardin was deeply involved in the very questionable
claim about the so-called "Peking Man."

Mr. Gould gives four reasons for the acceptance of
Piltdown Man by experts who would be expected to be
seeking scientific truth. He says these four reasons:

. . . contravene the usual mythology about scientific practice — that facts are hard and primary and that scientific understanding increases by patient collection and sifting of these object bits of pure information. Instead, they display science as a human activity, motivated by hope, cultural prejudice, and the pursuit of glory, yet stumbling in its erratic path toward a better understanding of nature.[7]

This is Mr. Gould's impression and teaching of what the so-called "science" of evolution is all about. It is contrary to the accepted scientific method which governs other scientific disciplines. We may learn from this event, these reactions of the evolutionists to it, and the comments and responses of a present-day leading academic evolutionist why the theory of evolution survives on misinformation and delusion. True scientific understanding does, indeed, increase by patient collection and sifting of objective bits of pure information. Hope, cultural prejudice, and the pursuit of glory produce lies.

### Nebraska Man

In 1922 a single molar tooth of great antiquity was discovered by Harold Cook in Nebraska. This fossilized tooth was proclaimed to be that of a half-ape and half-man. This imagined missing link was given the scientific name *Hesperopithecus haroldcookii* after its discoverer, and the *Illustrated London News* presented to the world a portrait of this creature. As usual, he was portrayed as being stooped and brutish. Evolutionists accepted *Nebraska Man* as an authentic ancestor of Homo sapiens who lived perhaps 500,000 years ago. His discovery was used in an attempt to discredit creationists in the Scopes Trial.

Nebraska Man was proven to be a figment of imagination when the lone tooth was shown to be that of an extinct pig in 1927. Nevertheless, he was still being used as evidence for the evolution of man in 1943.[8] The false claims of evolutionists are born with great fanfare, are taught with great authority, but die slowly and inconspicuously.

### Australopithecines

Evolutionists are now enamored with various primate finds categorized as *Australopithecines*. The first specimen, named *Australopithecus*, or southern ape, was found in 1924 in southern Africa. Other remains have been found since in Africa and elsewhere. While some evolutionists have been enthusiastic over the Australopithecines, these fossils have also stirred considerable debate within the camp.

Why are these relics thought to represent the missing link? Believing man is a product of evolution, paleoanthropologists appear to be searching for primates which may have walked upright and which may have used simple tools. The Australopithecines are claimed to fit these two criteria, but the requirements for bridging the gap between ape and man are difficult. These specimens fail the test.

First, even though they were bipedal (two-footed), a study of Australopithecines' structure shows that man's striding gait could not have evolved from them. This was the opinion of Dr. Charles E. Oxnard, professor of anatomy and anthropology at the University of Chicago. Oxnard and the university's Committee on Evolutionary Biology have conducted studies relating form and function of living and fossilized primates. Oxnard concluded "that these fossils are uniquely different from modern man in many major respects."[9]

For example, all non-human primates can run on all fours; man cannot.[10] The functions of the human hindlimb are different from those of non-human primates.[11] The shoulder of Australopithecines is "uniquely different from that of man,"[12] just as man's pelvis "is uniquely different from all other living species."[13]

Australopithecines were capable of climbing in ways that humans could only dream about. Their clavicles and scapulae (shoulder-area bones) were typical of animals that would regularly climb and hang by their upper limbs.[14] Other anatomical regions, such as the toe bones, suggest the Australopithecines were different functionally from both the humans and African apes of today.[15]

Oxnard, in fact, goes so far as to say that Australopithecines were neither ape nor human. From his perspective, they were bipedal primates, but on an evolutionary track separate from that of apes or humans.

Evolutionists disagree about which, if any, of the various Australopithecine species were directly ancestral to man. Paleoanthropologist Richard Leakey, for example, believes the genus *Homo*, to which man belongs, goes back five million years. Consequently, the younger and obviously different Australopithecines represent evolutionary dead-ends. Leakey believes a true transitional ancestor of man has not been found.

Donald Johanson, a paleoanthropologist, shares the frustration that no fossil has yet linked man with a direct ancestor. "Every specimen we have in hand is like a brushstroke on a canvas that has been bleached out, pulled to pieces, and scattered by the wind."[16]

Yet you would hardly suspect this paucity of evidence by reading contemporary material, whether pop-up books for children or academic compilations.

A 1988 children's book described how "new creatures appeared in the eastern part of Africa" three million years ago. How do new primates just "appear?" No clue. But now we call them Australopithecines. "In some ways they looked like apes; in other ways, like humans." The book, complete with three-dimensional illustrations, leaves the distinct impression that these creatures were the forerunners of man.[17]

Anthropologist Kathleen J. Reichs, editor of *Hominid Origins*, opened her 1988 book by assuring readers that, "The fossil record . . . now gives us a fascinating picture of the way we were as we evolved from the small-brained, large-toothed hunter-gatherers of the African savannah . . . ."[18] Read on, though, and the fascination appears a bit premature. Discussing the difficulty of pinpointing man's direct ancestor from fossil finds, she referred to "only a few tantalizing and fragmentary representatives of a period so critical in human evolution."[19] This, mind you, was after finding thousands of primate remains in Africa.

Reichs cited many authorities who disagree about the interpretations of these many discoveries. Until accurate dating of the finds is possible, she said, "reconstruction of hominid relationships must remain tenuous at best."[20]

### Endless Search

Even if we were to accept the possibility that these now extinct primates got around pretty effectively on their hind legs and used tools in simple ways as do some other animals, there remain differences that are much more profound.

To give apes their due, they can run twice as fast as man, and can use their arms in locomotion. They can travel through trees in ways that man (even Tarzan) cannot begin to imitate.

But the biggest physical gulf between us and apes is man's brain. It provides man with elaborate spoken and written language. It performs complex calculations, and can conceptualize things such as giant architectural complexes, personal computers and poetry. Obviously, man's brain power has enabled him to develop to levels of sophistication that dwarfs anything exhibited by apes or other animals. To anyone who believes in Genesis 1:28, man's ability to subdue and rule the earth comes as no surprise.

On a deeper level, the brain plays a part in recognizing moral values. Among these are altruism — an expression of self-sacrifice totally at odds with the survival of the fittest preached by evolution. The discovery of rudimentary communication and social structure among apes, as well as some other animals, in no way equates with the accomplishments of the human brain. The changes that would be required in DNA for ape brains to evolve to that of Homo sapiens are beyond comprehension.

The search for the missing link has shown early man to be an artisan and a tool maker. It has also shown that early apes were apes. If, indeed, there were a gradual transition from ape to man, there should be more of a clearly hominid trail of art and tools. There is none. The first archaeological evidences of man were left by complete men.

Darwin initially shied away from suggesting that man descended from apes. However, with *The Descent of Man* in 1870, he came clean. He argued that man, like all other species, came from a common progenitor. As with *The Origin of Species*, Darwin offered no proof to back up his opinions.

We still see varieties of primates today: lemurs, monkeys, chimpanzees, orangutans, gorillas, and others. If there was descent of any of these primates to man, why are allegedly "inferior" species still successful in their natural habitat? Why are the theorized intermediate, and presumably more adapted, species extinct? Why do we not find intermediate ape-men living in isolated enclaves today?

Evolutionists offer no satisfactory answers to these questions. It would seem that none of the fossil hunters or those who pass judgment on their claims are scientifically concerned about how evolution from beast to man is supposed to have occurred. Where is their molecular science? How did man's brain which God claims He created, come to be by some other creative force? DNA is never mentioned once in Leakey's and Lewin's book, *Origins*,[21] and it is once briefly mentioned in a footnote about "molecular clocks" in Johanson's *Lucy's Child*.[22]

Indeed, Leakey and Lewin unscientifically theorize: "The secret of human evolution is extreme adaptability, and the simple physical change that made this possible was the liberation of the hands from the basic function of locomotion."[23]

Evolutionists claim their theory is scientific. Where is the science? I can assure the reader the American Kennel Club would not certify an ancestor of your dog based on evidence such as paleontologists present.

[1]Stephen J. Gould, *The Panda's Thumb* (New York, London: W. W. Norton & Company, 1980), p. 110.

[2]Ibid., p. 114.

[3]Ibid., p. 115.

[4]Ibid., p. 114.

[5]Ibid., pp. 123-124.

[6]Ibid., p. 114.

[7]Ibid., pp. 115-116.

[8]S. E. Winbolt alluded to Nebraska Man as a genuine link in *Britain B. C.*, of the Pelican Book Series, according to R. L. Wysong, *The Creation Evolution Controversy* (Midland, Michigan: Inquiry Press, 1976), pp. 295-296.

[9]Charles E. Oxnard, *Uniqueness and Diversity in Human Evolution: Morphometric Studies of Australopithecines* (Chicago: University of Chicago Press, 1975), p. vii.

[10]Ibid., p. 27.

[11]Ibid., p. 33.

[12]Ibid., p. 45.

[13]Ibid., p. 63.

[14]Ibid., p. 179.

[15]Ibid., p. 180.

[16]Donald Johanson and James Shreeve, *Lucy's Child* (New York: William Morrow and Co., 1989), p. 280.

[17]Melvin Berger, *Early Humans: A Prehistoric World* (New York: G. P. Putnam's Sons, 1988), Michael Welpley, illus., inside cover.

[18]Kathleen J. Reichs, ed., *Hominid Origins* (Washington, DC: University Press of America, 1983), p. IX.

[19]Ibid., p. XIII.

[20]Ibid., p. XVIII.

[21]Richard E. Leakey and Roger Lewin, *Origins* (New York: E. P. Dutton, 1977).

[22]Johanson and Shreeve, op cit., p. 57.

[23]Leakey and Lewin, op. cit., p. 38.

# Biochemistry Says "God Made"

Evolutionists claim to represent the "scientific" approach to the origin of life and the development of kinds. Biblical claims that God created are declared by them to be pure religion which must and should rely totally on faith. Many theologians have knuckled under to this attack, and have tacitly agreed that science and religion should remain separate on this issue. If evolution had been shown to be true, if evolutionists had facts to back up their theories, then those of us who have experienced the presence of the living God would have no choice but to accept the first two chapters of Genesis as allegory. As I indicated in my introduction to *God Made*, I was prepared to do just that after being taught evolution as fact in medical school. I undertook my study of evolution to relate it to what I considered to be remarkably accurate allegory between something written 3,500 years ago and modern science.

However, there is a universal truth which would make the concept of the separation of God from science to be foolishness. If God is the Creator of the universe, all physical and biological laws must have been formulated by Him. Science would simply be a search for His truths. How, then, can religion and science be separated?

As pointed out in previous chapters, scientific information has tended to discount the theories of spontaneous origin of life and evolution of kinds. Embryology has failed to support the concepts, and so has comparative anatomy, genetics, the fossil record, and whatever else which might have supplied reliable objective evidence. The discovery of DNA as the code of life has made life nothing short of miraculous.

In Chapter 9, the organization of life was shown to be dependent on proteins. Some proteins are primarily building blocks of cells, and some are enzymatic machines which do the work of cells. Proteins are composed of amino acids, and a typical protein is made of several hundred to several thousand. These amino acids are arranged in very specific sequences dictated by the DNA which is the code specifying the production of the proteins in a cell. The sequences determine the three-dimensional (3-D) shape of each protein, and the function of a protein is determined by the 3-D shape. A single error in the sequence of amino acids can render a protein useless, detrimental or even fatal to an organism. Thus, instead of being accepted as the building blocks of evolution, random, chance mutations are recognized by authorities such as Nobel laureate H. J. Muller to be harmful.

Prior to the 1950s the perception of kinship of organisms was based solely on gross anatomical relationships. In 1957, X-ray crystallographic studies first demonstrated the 3-D structure of sperm whale *myoglobin*. Since then the 3-D structure of many proteins has been evaluated, and the exact sequence of amino acids composing these proteins can now be determined.

The sequence in any species is constant. Yet, proteins with similar characteristics and functions in different orders and kinds are found to vary in the sequence of amino acids.

The amino acid sequence of the same protein such as hemoglobin from two different organisms can be analyzed and the sequences compared. By counting the number of differing amino acids a numerical comparison can be made. A typical example of this comparison is as follows:

(1) G D V E K G K K I F I M K C S N C H T V
(2) G D V E E G K L I F V M K C A N D H T V
(Each capital letter stands for a particular amino acid)

In these two sequences there are five of twenty locations of amino acids which differ, representing a 25 percent difference. This numerical value of difference has been obtained for many different organisms, which include bacteria, fungi, higher plants, cyclostomes, bony fish, amphibians, reptiles, insects, birds, and mammals. M. O. Dayhoff has published comparative values of differences in a so-called "percent sequence difference" matrix (see Figure 1).[1] These have been carefully analyzed by Michael Denton, an Australian medical doctor and biological scientist, who discovered:

(1) Sequence differences can be used to "classify" organisms. Interestingly, the groups thus derived turn out to correspond to traditional groups arrived at years ago by anatomic methods.[2]

(2) Sequence differences become greater as taxonomic (classification) distance increases. Thus there is less divergence between two mammals than between a mammal and a fish.[3]

(3) Each subclass is isolated and distinct.[4]

(4) No sequence or group of organisms can be designated as intermediate with respect to other groups. None can be recognized as being more primitive than another.[5]

(5) Despite these differences among groups, the astonishing observation is made that all eukaryotes (organisms which reproduce sexually and have a nucleus within the cell) are equally divergent from bacteria which reproduce asexually by simple cell division and are known as prokaryotes. Thus, unicelled organisms such as yeast exhibit the same numerical sequence divergence from bacteria as does man, whale, chicken, fish, insect, or even higher plants. There is nothing in these comparative amino acid sequences among biological proteins to indicate any evolutionary pathway from bacteria to any other form of life. It is as though all were carefully engineered with proteins containing their own unique amino acid sequences.[6]

If the theory of Darwin or any other theory of evolution were true, the tabulation of protein sequences should offer a clear, mathematically precise method of demonstrating transitional forms at the molecular level.

Evolutionists were hopeful that the biological relationships of organisms could be shown to have progressed from "simple life" such as bacteria along the lines of a "phylogenetic tree" to ever higher forms. *Biochemistry* was expected to reveal the "missing links" which have been persistently denied by the *fossil record.*

Instead, this modern biochemistry has dealt another mortal blow to the theory of evolution. It has confirmed what has been apparent in anatomical classification: that groups appear to be well defined and isolated with no evidence of transitional forms. Bacteria, yeasts, plants, insects, mammals, birds, reptiles, amphibians, fish, and cyclostomes are separate and distinct. There is no evidence in the biochemistry of cells that any group of organisms is more primitive than another, nor that any group is ancestral to another.

Michael Denton points out that when minor subdivisions of the animal kingdom such as primates are analyzed for protein sequential differences the same non-overlapping matrix is apparent. Thus, among monkeys, gibbons, apes, and man, all are separate and distinct with no hint of transition from one species to another.[8]

DNA is the blueprint for protein production, and as expected, sequence differences in the DNA of different species of organisms are found. When compared, similar non-overlapping results are apparent.[9]

**Fig. 1**

Matrix of Cytochromes Percent Sequence Difference (from Dayhoff).[7]

| | Human | Pig | Dog | Grey Whale | Pekin Duck | Snapping Turtle | Rattlesnake | Bullfrog | Tuna | Dogfish | Lamprey | Fruit Fly | Castor | Wheat | Baker's Yeast | Rhodospirillum rubrum $C_2$ |
|---|---|---|---|---|---|---|---|---|---|---|---|---|---|---|---|---|
| Human | 0 | | | | | | | | | | | | | | | |
| Pig | 10 | 0 | | | | | | | | | | | | | | |
| Dog | 11 | 3 | 0 | | | | | | | | | | | | | |
| Grey Whale | 10 | 2 | 3 | 0 | | | | | | | | | | | | |
| Pekin Duck | 11 | 8 | 8 | 7 | 0 | | | | | | | | | | | |
| Snapping Turtle | 14 | 9 | 9 | 8 | 7 | 0 | | | | | | | | | | |
| Rattlesnake | 13 | 19 | 20 | 18 | 16 | 21 | 0 | | | | | | | | | |
| Bullfrog | 17 | 11 | 12 | 11 | 11 | 10 | 23 | 0 | | | | | | | | |
| Tuna | 20 | 16 | 17 | 16 | 16 | 17 | 25 | 10 | 0 | | | | | | | |
| Dogfish | 23 | 15 | 16 | 15 | 16 | 18 | 25 | 19 | 14 | 0 | | | | | | |
| Lamprey | 19 | 13 | 13 | 14 | 17 | 18 | 26 | 18 | 19 | 16 | 0 | | | | | |
| Fruit Fly | 27 | 22 | 21 | 22 | 22 | 22 | 29 | 23 | 24 | 24 | 27 | 0 | | | | |
| Castor | 37 | 38 | 38 | 38 | 38 | 38 | 38 | 38 | 42 | 43 | 41 | 41 | 0 | | | |
| Wheat | 38 | 40 | 39 | 39 | 41 | 41 | 42 | 40 | 42 | 43 | 45 | 42 | 12 | 0 | | |
| Baker's Yeast | 41 | 41 | 41 | 41 | 41 | 44 | 44 | 43 | 44 | 45 | 46 | 41 | 41 | 42 | 0 | |
| Rhodospirillum rubrum $C_2$ | 65 | 64 | 65 | 65 | 64 | 64 | 64 | 65 | 65 | 65 | 65 | 65 | 66 | 66 | 69 | 0 |

Because a single mistranscribed amino acid can cause serious malfunction of a protein, the different sequences discovered between different species would appear to have been very carefully conceived by an intelligence which knew all about what he was doing. If helpful mutations occurred in the proteins of individuals of established orders one would expect to find sequence differences within the same species. In Dayhoff's matrix of cytochrome sequence differences no such divergence is found. This may indicate that the differences observed between different classes of organisms were not due to mutations, but rather to differences created at a moment in time followed by stability.

Contrary to what one would expect if evolution were true, Dayhoff's data indicates:[10]

(1)   The snapping turtle is slightly closer to a pig or dog than to a bullfrog, and it is much closer to all of these than to a dogfish or lamprey eel.

(2)   A fruit fly is as close to a human as it is to a rattlesnake or a lamprey eel.

(3)   Baker's yeast is as close to a human as it is to a monkey, pig, whale, tuna fish, or fruit fly. It is as close to these as it is to a castor bean.

(4)   The bacterium Rhodospirillum rubrum $C_2$ is as close to a human as it is to yeast, wheat, a dogfish, or a duck.

This very modern scientific technique shows that all forms of life are separate and distinct kinds. There is no evidence that any kind has gradually changed into another kind. Where is the scientific basis for evolution? How can the claim be established that evolution is "the scientific method?" Modern scientific, molecular evidence has joined hands with fossil evidence to proclaim the truth of Genesis, that God created "after their kinds."

Dr. Michael Denton states: "There is little doubt that if this molecular evidence had been available one century ago it would have been seized upon with devastating effect by the opponents of evolution theory like Agassiz and Owen, and the idea of organic evolution might never have been accepted."[11]

[1]Margaret O. Dayhoff, *Atlas of Protein Sequence and Structure* (Washington, DC: National Biomedical Research Foundation, Georgetown University Medical Center, 1972), vol. 5, Matrix 1, D-8.
[2]Michael Denton, *Evolution: A Theory in Crisis* (Bethesda, MD: Adler and Adler, Publishers, Inc., 1986), p. 278.
[3]Ibid., p. 278.
[4]Ibid., pp. 278-279.
[5]Ibid., p. 286.
[6]Ibid., p. 280.
[7]Dayhoff, op. cit., D-8.
[8]Denton, op. cit., p. 287.
[9]Ibid.
[10]Dayhoff, op. cit., D-8.
[11]Denton, op. cit., pp. 290-291.

# Why Fight It?

The book of Genesis establishes the foundation of Christian doctrine and theology. Jesus referred to this Scripture as a supporting authority for several of His teachings. It is referred to in the New Testament more than any other book of the Old Testament. Those who seek to undermine Christianity attack not only the tenets of the Church, but the very foundation which is the Word. Genesis is the book most vehemently attacked.

Jesus said in John 8:12, "I am the light of the world: he that followeth me shall not walk in darkness, but shall have the light of life." Yet evolutionist Theodosius Dobzhansky quotes Pierre Teilhard de Chardin, who may have been involved in the Piltdown Man scandal, as claiming: "Evolution is a light which illuminates all facts, a trajectory which all lines of thought must follow."[1]

Despite the overwhelming lack of scientific confirmation of the theory of evolution and the complete lack of any clue as to how life could have begun without a Creator, evolution is credited in our schools and in our press as representing pure science, whereas belief in

God as Creator is relegated to represent pure religion. I hope this book has helped to demonstrate the fallibility of this claim. Evolution is believed and taught on faith, and to some it is. The word "evolve" has come to be the semantic replacement for "create" in all reports in scientific journals and most lay press.

A. E. Wilder-Smith, who not only taught science in several European universities, but with his wife raised several children, wrote:

In the United States and Western European countries where scientific materialism has often laid hold of the younger generation, the following pattern is often observed: The teenage son or daughter, brought up in a sincere, religious family . . . is to be prepared for a position of leadership. For this he needs higher education . . . . Let us say that our student chooses science as his field.

During his freshman year he rapidly discovers, as a result of the scientific materialism which is the basis of all scientific higher education today, that the whole supernatural structure of belief on which the stability and happiness of his family rested during his formative years, was just nonsense. If our student had been brought up in a Christian family he rapidly finds, for example, that the family Bible allegedly contains a mere collection of myths on creation, the flood, the prophets, and the life of Jesus Christ. Today's science teaches that human life did not arise with Adam and Eve. Rather, "pools of interbreeding genes" would allegedly better describe the scientific facts of our ancestry.[2]

If you are a parent or a student, I suspect you are familiar with the situation Dr. Wilder-Smith described.

We have "evolved" in the United States to the position of allowing only the evolutionary doctrine to be taught in public institutions of learning. Unfortunately, many of our churches fail to emphasize the truth of Creation. Henry M. Morris, Ph.D., president of the Institute for Creation Research, has said: "The great need of the Christian church today is revival . . . from apathy and compromise."[3]

I have already admitted that I was led to accept evolution by teachers who taught it as factually sound. There are many who have been thus convinced, and the teaching goes on. It is an insidiously dangerous concept. It may be the principle basis for the popular liberal theology which has permeated the church. Ken Ham, who has written eloquently of the anti-Christian dangers of evolution in *The Lie: Evolution,* quotes Josef Ton, who was pastor of the largest Baptist church in Romania, as stating: "I came to the conclusion that there were two factors which destroyed Christianity in Western Europe. One was the theory of evolution and the other liberal theology . . . . Liberal theology is just evolution applied to the Bible and our faith."[4]

Ham also quoted James and Marti Helfley writing in *By Their Blood: Christian Martyrs of the 20th Century.*

New philosophies and theologies from the West also helped to erode Chinese confidence in Christianity. A new wave of so-called missionaries from main-line Protestant denominations came teaching evolution and a non-supernatural view of the Bible. Methodist, Presbyterian, Congregational and Northern Baptist schools were especially hard hit. Bertrand Russell came from England preaching atheism and socialism. Destructive books brought by such teachers further undermined orthodox Christianity. The Chinese intelligentsia who had been schooled by orthodox evangelical missionaries were thus softened for the advent of Marxism. Evolution is destroying the church and society today, and Christians need to be awakened to that fact.[5]

Evolution manifests its evils in social as well as religious ways. Communism is fundamentally atheistic, and its very foundation rests upon evolution. Karl Marx desired to dedicate his book, *Das Kapital*, to Charles Darwin, but Darwin refused. Hitler was an enthusiastic believer in evolution and was bold enough to apply its principles to the Nazi dogma. These principles were basic to his concept of the superiority of the Aryan stock, and his horrible program of extermination of what he considered "inferior" races and individuals.

### *Absolute Authority Versus Evolving Morals*

If evolution explains man's origins, then Genesis 1 is mere allegory. If we cannot believe the first chapter of the Bible, we cannot give much credence to the rest of it. If God's revealed Word is erroneous in matters as basic as creation of the world, His authority comes into question.

When God, through His agent, the church, loses authority, the void will not last long. Nature (the unseen hand of evolution), man (the pinnacle of evolution), and the state (collective man) are some of the common idols that rise to the surface in God's absence. When men fail to acknowledge the Bible as law, they are quick to make their own law. We allow evolution to erode biblical authority at our own peril.

When Oliver Wendell Holmes, Jr., wrote in *The Common Law* in 1881 that, "The life of the law has been . . . experience," he translated Darwinism into his own judicial philosophy. Holmes, who was to become a renowned Supreme Court Justice, believed that law should evolve along with the norms of society. The progressive interpretation of law should be based on man.

Holmes's outlook typifies our view of law and authority today. Society increasingly sees no legal/moral absolutes because times are changing — evolving — and only the fuddy-duddies refuse to change with them. Consequently, it becomes harder and harder to speak with any authority against social ills that used to be taboo under traditional Judeo-Christian ethics: abortion, divorce, drug abuse, pre-marital sex, adultery, and homosexuality. Those who formerly had unquestioned authority to address these issues — parents, ministers, and teachers — likewise have trouble mustering respect because their foundation for authority is attacked.

In some of these areas, evolutionary philosophy itself wars against traditional Christian beliefs. God's plan for family as presented in Genesis 2:24 begins with the uniting of man and woman. Yet under today's liberal ethics, the concept of family is evolving. Any two consenting adults — even homosexual or lesbian couples — are urged by some to qualify as a family and receive appropriate recognition and benefits. Even more atrocious is the application of evolution's survival of the fittest to the right to life. One of the chief arguments for legal abortion is that some lives are not worth living or they are simply inconvenient.

### Humanistic Philosophy

The second area where modern thought has lined up with evolution concerns humanism. If man, without the aid of God, has slimed his way out of the primordial soup and diligently climbed the evolutionary ladder over these millions of years, then who knows where he will stop? Poverty, disease, ignorance, and waste may be all too evident, but if man is constantly evolving, he can fashion an ever more perfect world.

In the words of classical humanism, Pythagoras wrote in the fifth century B.C., "Man is the measure of all things." That still applied when humanism enjoyed its revival in Europe in the 1300s to the 1500s. Humanists began to exalt man, his potential, and his innate goodness (as opposed to church teaching on sinfulness). This led to the Renaissance, when man's abilities and creativity were celebrated as never before.

Though evolution was not an issue then, residual humanism neatly absorbed evolution in the nineteenth and twentieth centuries. As humanism resurged in this century as secular humanism — a militantly anti-religious (and anti-creationist) dogma — it proclaimed not just man as good, but man as messiah. No deity will save mankind, secular humanists aver; we must save ourselves.

Instead of believing, "With God, all things are possible," they believe, "Without God, all things are possible." All things are especially possible through man's elite corps, the intellectuals and state planners, the distillation of millennia of evolution. Secular humanism exalts these illuminati as having the answers for the rest of us, especially those who blindly follow what they consider "mythical" Christianity, which has committed the humanists' version of mortal sin: failure to evolve.

Julian Huxley, atheist and rabid evolutionist, has proposed, "Evolutionary Humanism" as a new religion. He wrote:

> The word "religion" is often used restrictively to mean belief in gods, but I am not using it in this sense . . . I am using it in a broader sense, to denote an overall relation between man and his destiny, and one involving his deepest feelings, including his sense of what is sacred. In this broad sense, evolutionary humanism, it seems to me, is capable of becoming the germ of a new religion . . . .[6]

Do you see evidence in present day conflicts within our churches of the influence of the so-called Evolutionary Humanists? According to Huxley:

> . . . Evolutionary Humanism is necessarily unitary instead of dualistic, affirming the unity of mind and body, . . . naturalistic instead of supernaturalist. . . . It will have nothing to do with Absolutes, including absolute truth, absolute morality, absolute perfection, and absolute authority, but insists that we can find standards to which our actions and our aims can properly be related.[7]

### Rebellion and Reconciliation

All the political movements and philosophies that lean on evolution, all the humanistic exaltations of the individual and his right to do whatever he pleases in a climate where moral absolutes died off in the Pre-Cambrian era, can be summed up in one word: *rebellion.*

Genesis wastes little time before addressing the same subject. God's first generation of species made in His image rebelled. In a sense, the attitude of Adam and Eve in Genesis 3 was no different than the attitudes of those today who find themselves freed from any link to the divine: They all declare an authority separate from God. Adam and Eve suffered the consequences of choosing their own lordship. Our society is likewise suffering today for our choosing self-indulgence as exemplified by the AIDS and venereal disease epidemics, child abuse, suicide, substance abuse, marital infidelity, and rampant divorce.

As we have seen, there are two paths to follow in understanding God's creation, each with its own light. These can be seen in the same two choices described by Elijah to a rebellious and idolatrous crowd on Mount Carmel. Each path has its distinct outcome. Isaiah advised taking only one: "Who is among you that feareth the Lord, that obeyeth the voice of his servant, that walketh in darkness, and hath no light? let him trust in the name of the Lord, and stay upon his God" (Isaiah 50:10).

He also warned those who would fancy themselves pathfinders at the expense of God's revelation: "Behold, all ye that kindle a fire, that compass yourselves about with sparks: walk in the light of your fire, and in the sparks that ye have kindled. This shall ye have of mine hand; ye shall lie down in sorrow" (Isaiah 50:11).

Evolution, Teilhard de Chardin said, "is a light which illuminates all facts." But who struck the match for this lantern? Who has stoked the flame of evolution into a blazing torch? A group of scientists and would-be scientists have ignited this fiery doctrine and carried the torch before a generally gullible, often apathetic public.

Christians, however, can no longer ignore this attack on God, His authority, and His Word. Darwin's imaginative musings have permeated the halls of education and society at large. If we accept the claims of pseudoscience as superior or too difficult to challenge, we demean the value and authority of God's Word. We place ourselves subject to the same sanctions God promises for all those who light their torches and walk by false light.

My hope in exposing only some of the flaws in evolutionary theory is that our eyes will be opened to the facts of God's creation. I desire that Christians will see that God *made*, rather than God *allowed to evolve*. The King of the Universe exercised His sovereignty in creating the world and its organisms. Recognizing this truth not only does not contradict science, as many textbooks and media stories would have us believe, but much to the contrary, it helps us to understand the special order of creation that science continues to confirm.

The unfolding revelations of science — showing that kinds, although exhibiting variations of species, are clearly fixed — should work together with Scripture to give us comfort in God's complete plan. Psalm 139:14-16 reassures us: "I will praise thee; for I am fearfully and wonderfully made: marvelous are thy works; and that my soul knoweth right well. My substance was not hidden from thee when I was made in secret, and curiously wrought in the lowest parts of the earth. Thine eyes did see my substance, yet being unperfect [or unformed]; and in thy book all my members were written, which in continuance were fashioned, when as yet there was none of them."

[1]Theodosius Dobzhansky, *The American Biology Teacher*, Vol. 35, No. 3, March 1973, 129.
[2]A. E. Wilder-Smith, *The Creation of Life* (San Diego, CA: Master Books, Division of CLP Publishers, 1981), p. 15.

[3]Henry M. Morris, *Creation and the Modern Christian* (El Cajon, CA: Master Book Publishers, 1985), p. 12.

[4]Kenneth A. Ham, *The Lie: Evolution* (El Cajon, CA: Creation-Life Publishers, Master Books Division, 1987), p. 105.

[5]Ibid.

[6]Julian Huxley, *Evolution in Action* (New York: Harper Brothers, 1953), p. 171.

[7]Huxley, *Essays of a Humanist* (New York and Evanston: Harper & Row Publishers, 1964), pp. 73-74.

# Glossary

*Abiogenesis* — Spontaenous generation of life from non-living matter.

*Adrenal Glands* — Paired endocrine glands located just above mammalian kidneys; involved in controlling water/salt balance and physiological reactions to stress.

*Aerodynamics* — The science of air and gases in motion.

*Algae* — Simple, mostly aquatic, organisms, including the seaweed and many unicellular fresh-water plants, most of which contain chlorophyll.

*Amino Acid* — Organic compounds containing an amino group ($-NH_2$) and a carboxyl group ($-COOH$) both bonded to the same carbon atom.

*Ammonite* — Any of numerous flat spiral fossil shells of cephalopods, especially abundant in what geologists consider ancient strata.

*Amphibia* — A class of vertebrate animals that breathe by means of gills in the larval state, but after metamorphosis, breathe by means of lungs. It includes frogs, toads, newts, and salamanders.

*Analgesia* — Absence of sensibility to pain.

*Analogous* — Resembling or similar in some respects, as in function or appearance, but not in origin or development.

*Anemia* — A condition in which the blood is deficient in

red blood cells, in hemoglobin, or in total volume.

*Anthropology* — The study of human beings in relation to distribution, origin, classification, and relationship of races, physical character, environmental and social relations, and culture.

*Antibiotic* — A substance able in dilute solution to inhibit or kill a microorganism.

*Archaeology* — The scientific study of material remains of past human life and activities.

*Archaeopteryx* — A fossilized bird discovered in Germany in the nineteenth century thought by evolutionists to be a transition between reptile and bird; now considered to be a fully formed bird of flight.

*Archipelago* — A group of islands.

*Asteroid* — One of thousands of small planets between Mars and Jupiter with diameters from a fraction of a mile to nearly five hundred miles.

*Atheist* — One who denies the existence of God.

*ATP* — Adenine Triphosphate. A compound occurring in all living cells involved in the storage and release of energy.

*Austrolopithecus* — An extinct southern African ape.

*Avian* — Of, or pertaining to, birds.

*Bacterium* — Unicellular prokaryotic microorganisms living in soil, water, organic matter, or the bodies of plants and animals.

*Barbule* — A minute barb which fringes the barbs of a feather.

*Beta-lactamase* — Enzymes produced by some bacteria which inhibit the action of some antibiotics, such as Penicillin.

*Biogenesis* — The development of life from pre-existing life.

*BTU* — British thermal unit: The quantity of heat required to raise the temperature of one pound of water one degree Fahrenheit at or near 39.2° F.

*Calcareous* — Containing calcium.

*Cambrian* — Of, or relating to, what geologists consider to be the earliest geologic system of rocks containing fossils of every great animal type except the vertebrate.

*Carbohydrate* — Any of various compounds of carbon, hydrogen, and oxygen (Sugars, starches, cellulose), formed by green plants, and which constitute a major class of animal foods.

*Cell membrane* — A cell wall.

*Cellulose* — A complex carbohydrate constituting the chief part of the cell walls of plants.

*Cephalosporin* — A broad-spectrum antibiotic.

*Chlorophyll* — The green coloring matter of plants within the cells of plants, and being the seat of photosynthesis.

*Chromatic* — Of, or relating to color.

*Chromosome* — A structure in the nucleus containing a linear thread of DNA which transmits genetic information. Each organism of a species is characterized by the same number of chromosomes, 46 being the number normally present in man.

*Cilium* — A hair-like process of some cells that is capable of a lashing movement.

*Clone* — An asexual progeny of a single cell.

*Cold-blooded* — Having a body temperature not internally regulated and approximating that of the environment. Also ectothermic. Opposite of endothermic.

*Colloid* — A mixture composed of insoluble particles that remain suspended within a fluid and do not settle out.

*Cosmic ray* — A stream of atomic nuclei of extremely penetrating character that enter the earth's atmosphere from outer space at speeds approaching that of light.

*Crustacea* — Mostly aquatic anthropods having an exoskeleton and including lobsters, shrimps, crabs, wood lice, water fleas, and barnacles.

*Cutaneous* — Relating to the skin.

*Cyclostome* — Any of a class of vertebrates having a large sucking mouth with no jaws and comprising the hagfishes and lampreys.

*Cytoplasm* — The protoplasm of a cell exclusive of the nucleus, containing the organelles; the site of most of the chemical activities of the cell.

*DNA (Deoxyribonucleic acid)* — A nucleic acid that functions as the genetic material of all living organisms, both plants and animals; composed of two complimentary strands of nucleotides coiled together into a double helix.

*Diaphragm* — A sheet music-like muscle separating the thoracic cavity from the abdominal cavity; functions in filling and emptying the lungs by its contractions.

*Drosophila* — Any of a genus of small two-winged flies extensively used in the study of inheritance and mutation. Commonly called "fruit flies."

*Electron Microscope* — A microscope in which a beam of electrons focused by means of an electron lens is used to produce an enlarged image of extremely minute objects on a photographic plate.

*Endoplasmic reticulum* — A network of microtubules and vesicles within eukaryotic cells. See chapter 9.

*Endorphins* — A group of opiate-like hormones produced in the brain that act as natural painkillers.

*Enkephalins* — Pentapeptides (Five amino acids) produced in the brain, spinal cord, nerve plexuses, and glands of the intestines. They function as neuromodulators in the brain and spinal cord and are involved with pain perception, movement, mood, behavior, and neuroendocrine regulation.

*Entrophy* — A quantitative measure of disorder.

*Enzyme* — A protein catalyst that controls the speed and direction of chemical reactions within living organisms without being used up by the reaction.

*Eukaryote* — An organism whose cells contain a nucleus. All animals are eukaryotic and all plants except bacteria and blue-green algae.

*Extraterrestrial* — Originating or existing outside the earth or its atmosphere.

*Fibroblast* — A connective tissue cell.

*Fluorine* — A non-metallic element that is normally a pale, yellowish gas.

*Fossil* — Any remains, impression or trace of an animal or plant that has been preserved in the earth's crust.

*Fungus* — Any of a major group of saprophytic and parasitic plants that lack chlorophyll and include molds, rusts, mildews, smuts, and mushrooms.

*Gene* — The basic hereditary unit composed of a sequence of DNA on a chromosome. One gene typically codes for one protein.

*Globulin* — Any of a class of simple proteins insoluble in

pure water, but soluble in dilute salt solutions.

*Glucose* — A simple sugar which is produced by plants and is readily assimilated as an energy source by animals. It occurs only in dextrorotary form in living organisms.

*Golgi Complex* — A membrane-bound organelle that funtions in processing, packaging, distributing, and secreting proteins.

*Gymnotus* — A genus of the Gymnotidae, a family of South American fish, that includes the electric eel.

*Helix* — Something spiral in form.

*Hemoglobin* — An iron containing protein respiratory pigment occurring in the red blood cells of animals.

*Homeostasis* — A stable state of equilibrium between the interdependent elements of an organism.

*Homologous* — A term for fundamentally similar organs or structures modified to serve dissimilar ends.

*Hormone* — An organic compound produced in one part of an organism, and transported to another part, where it produces a specific effect on the activity of cells.

*Humanism* — A system or attitude of the thought based on human interests and ideals rather than religious principles, holding that man's nature is perfectible through his own efforts without divine grace.

*Hypothalamus* — A region of the vertebrate midbrain that funtions in regulating homeostasis, emotions, the autonomic nervous system, and the pituitary gland.

*Infrared rays* — Thermal radiation of wavelengths longer than those of visible light.

*Insect* — One of a class of invertebrate animals, often having wings, but always having bodies composed of compartmentalized head, thorax and abdomen, with three pairs of jointed legs.

*Invertebrate* — An animal lacking a spinal column.

*Ion* — An atom that carries a positive or negative electric charge as a result of having gained or lost one or more electrons.

*Labellum* — The median member of the corolla of an orchid.

*Lichen* — A complex thallophytic plant made up of an alga and a fungus growing in symbiotic association on a solid surface.

*Lipids* — Organic compounds that are insoluble in water including oils, fats, phospholipids, and waxes. Some are components of cell membranes, and act as long-term storage forms of energy.

*Lysosome* — An intracellular organelle containing digestive enzymes.

*Macroevolution* — Major evolutionary change supposed by evolutionists to result in the formation of new species and kinds.

*Mammal* — Vertebrate animals that nourish their young with milk secreted by mammary glands. Their skin is usually covered with hair.

*Mammary glands* — Special paired glands of origin which produce milk and usually terminate in a nipple.

*Meiosis* — A type of nuclear division occurring only in organisms that reproduce sexually, involving two successive nuclear divisions, resulting in the number of chromosomes being reduced to one half the normal number.

*Metabolic* — Relating to metabolism.

*Metabolism* — The sum total of all chemical reactions occurring in an organism, both catabolic and anabolic.

*Meteroid* — A meteor particle.

*Microbiologist* — A scientist who studies microorganisms.

*Microevolution* — Evolutionary change resulting from minute variations.

*Microorganism* — An organism of microscopic or ultra-microscopic size.

*Microtubule* — Hollow rods of protein that make up portions of the cytoskeleton including organelles.

*Mitochondria* — Organelles in which respiration takes place; often referred to as the "powerhouse" of the cell. Contain most of the ATP in the cell.

*Mitosis* — A type of asexual division involving the replication and distribution of identical chromosomes to each of two daughter cells.

*Molecule* — A chemical unit consisting of two or more atoms held together by ionic or covalent bonds.

*Mollusca* — Invertebrate animals with a soft unsegmented body usually enclosed in a calcareous shell (Shellfish, such as clams and snails.)

*Mutation* — Change in genetic material (DNA).

*Neo-Darwinism* — The synthesis of Darwin's original hypothesis with newer discoveries of genetics and discarding his claims of acquired characteristics.

*Nucleotide* — An organic molecule consisting of a five-carbon sugar (either ribose or deoxyribose), a nitrogenous base, and a phosphate group.

*Nucleus* — An organelle containing DNA: often referred to as the control center of the cell. Present only in eukaryotic cells (except mature red blood cells).

*Opiate* — A preparation or derivitive of opium. A narcotic analgesic.

*Optical* — Relating to vision.

*Organelle* — A specialized membrane-bound structure within cells that performs a specific function.

*Organic* — Relating to chemistry of carbon compounds of living beings, and most other carbon compounds.

*Osmosis* — The movement of water across a semipermeable membrane, tending to equal the concentrations of solutions.

*Ozone* — $O_3$ or "heavy oxygen."

*Ozone shield* — A layer of ozone in the upper atmosphere of earth which shields the earth from much ultraviolet light.

*Paleontology* — The study of fossils.

*Parabronchi* — Tertiary, very small bronchial tubes in the lungs of birds which serve not only as air passages, but for gaseous exchange.

*Pathologist* — One who studies and interprets the changes in tissues caused by disease.

*Pencillinase* — An enzyme secreted by some organisms which inactives penicillin.

*Periosteum* — The membrane of connective tissue that closely invests all bones except at joint surfaces.

*Phagocytosis* — The engulfing and usually destruction of particulate matter by cells.

*Phosphate* — A salt or ester of phosphoric acid.

*Photosynthesis* — Formation of carbohydrates from water and carbon dioxide in the chlorophyll-containing tissues of plants by the energy or sunlight.

*Phylogeny* — The proposed evolutionary history of a species or group of organisms.

*Physical* — Of, or relating to, the body.

*Physiology* — The study of the functions and processes performed by organisms.

*Pituitary gland* — A small endocrine gland at the base of the brain whose secreted hormones help to regulate the activities of many body tissues and of several other endocrine glands.

*Plasmid* — A circular segment of DNA found in prokaryotic cells that carries genes separate from those on main chromosomes; capable of independent replication and transfer to other prokaryotes. Important in transfer of bacterial resistance to antibiotics.

*Pollen* — The mature microgametophyte of seed plants consisting of a haploid tube nucleus and two haploid sperm nuclei.

*Polysaccharide* — A long chained carbohydrate made of three or more monosaccharides, such as starch, cellulose, and glycogen; all of which are made of many monosaccharides.

*Precambrian* — The earliest era of geological history.

*Precipitate* — A substance separated out of solution or suspension.

*Primate* — Any of an order of mammals comprising man together with apes, monkeys, gorillas, lemurs, etc.

*Progenitor* — A biologically ancestral form.

*Prokaryote* — An organism lacking a nucleus, and which reproduces asexually by mitosis. Includes bacteria and blue-green algae.

*Protein* — A 3-D micromolecule made of amino acids, all

of which are L-forms. Primary constituents of all plant and animal cells.

*Prototype* — An original model on which something is patterned.

*Punctuated equilibrium* — A theory of evolutionary change that suggests that long periods of no change are interrupted by rapid bursts of change. Opposite of Darwin's gradualism.

*Radar* — A radio system for locating and analyzing an object by means of ultrahigh-frequency radio waves reflected from the object and received.

*Radiation* — Energy radiated in the form of waves or particles.

*Radioactive* — Exhibiting radioactivity, spontaneously emitting alpha or beta, or sometimes gamma rays by the disintegration of the nuclei of atoms, such as uranium.

*Ray* — Any of numerous elasmobranch fishes (order Hypotremata) having the body flattened dorsoventrally, the eyes on the upper surface, and a much reduced caudal region.

*Replication* — The act or process of reproducing.

*Reptile* — Airbreathing vertebrates including alligators, crocodiles, lizards, snakes, and turtles, having a completely ossified skeleton and a body usually covered with scales or bony plates.

*Ribonucleic acid (RNA)* — A nucleic acid that is produced by transcription from the DNA composing a gene, but being composed of a single strand of nucleotides, and functioning in the production of proteins from amino acids.

*Semipermeable* — The physical and chemical property of

biological membranes that allows some substances such as water and small ions to pass through more easily than large molecules.

*Sequence* — An orderly arrangement of elements.

*Sonar* — An apparatus that detects the presence of a submerged object by means of reflected sound waves.

*Speciation* — The differentiation of new species.

*Species* — A category of biological classification comprising related organisms potentially capable of interbreeding.

*Specific heat* — The heat in calories required to raise the temperature of one gram of a substance one degree centigrade.

*Stratum* — A layer in which archaeological material (as artifacts, skeletons, dwelling remains) is found on excavation.

*Swimbladder* — The air bladder of a fish.

*Symbiosis* — The intimate living together of two dissimilar organisms in a mutually beneficial relationship.

*Synthetic theory* — Neo-Darwin theory of evolution which includes the synthesis of change by mutation with natural selection applied over long periods of time.

*T-cell (T lymphocyte)* — "T" refers to thymus, the gland located just above the heart in which these cells mature. A white blood cell that directly attacks and destroys foreign substances, cells, or tissues (cell-mediated immunity).

*Taxonomy* — Classification of organisms into categories, such as species, genera, families, orders, classes, and phyla.

*Terrarium* — A vivarium without standing water.

*Terrestrial* — Of, or relating to, the earth or its inhabitants.

*Theist* — Believer in God.

*Thermodynamics* — Physics which deals with the mechanical action or relations of heat.

*Toxin* — A colloidal, proteinaceous poisonous substance produced by an organism.

*Transmutation* — An act or instance of change or alteration in form, appearance, or nature.

*Ultraviolet ray* — Light ray having a wavelength shorter than visible light, and longer than those of X-rays.

*Unicelled organism* — An organism consisting of a single cell.

*Vertebrate* — Having a vertebral column; includes fishes, amphibians, reptiles, birds, and mammals.

*Vivarium* — An enclosure containing living plants and animals.

*Water vapor* — Water in gaseous form.

# Suggested Reading

Darwin, Charles. *The Origin of Species by Means of Natural Selection.*

Davis, P., D. H. Kenyon, C. B. Thaxton. *Of Pandas and People.* Dallas: Houghton Publishing Co., 1989.

Denton, Michael. *Evolution. A Theory in Crisis.* Bethesda, MD: Adler & Adler, Inc., 1986.

Gentry, Robert V. *Creation's Tiny Mystery.* Knoxville, TN: Birth Science Assoc., 1986.

Gish, Duane T. *Evolution, the Challenge of the Fossil Record.* El Cajon, CA: Creation-Life Publishers, Master Books Division, 1985.

——————. *Evolution, the Fossils Say No!* San Diego: Creation-Life Publishers, 1973.

Johnson, Phillip E. *Darwin on Trial.* Washington: Regnery Gateway, 1991.

Morris, Henry M. *Creation and the Modern Christian.* El Cajon, CA: Master Book Publishers, 1985.

Morris, Henry M. and Gary E. Parker. *What is Creation*

*Science?* San Diego: Creation-Life Publishers, Inc., 1982.

Rusch, Wilbert H., Sr. and John W. Klontz. Edited by Emmett L. Williams: *Did Charles Darwin Become a Christian?* Norcross, GA: Creation Research Society Books, 1988.

Rusch, Wilbert H., Sr. *The Argument. Creationism vs. Evolutionism.* Norcross, GA: Creation Research Society Monography Series No. 3.

Sunderland, Luther D. *Darwin's Enigma.* Santee, CA: Master Book Publishers, 1984.

Thaxton, C. B., W. L. Bradley, and R. L. Olsen. *The Mystery of Life's Origin.* Dallas: Lewis & Stanley Publishers, 1984.

Whitcomb, John C. and Henry M. Morris. *The Genesis Flood.* Phillipsburg, NJ: Presbyterian and Reformed Publishing Co., 1961.

Wilder-Smith, A. E. *Man's Origin, Man's Destiny.* Minneapolis: Bethany Fellowship, Inc., 1975.

_____. *The Creation of Life.* San Diego: Master Books, 1981.

_____. *The Natural Sciences Know Nothing of Evolution.* San Diego: Master Books, 1981.

_____. *The Scientific Alternative to Neo-Darwinian*

*Evolutionary Theory*. Costa Mesa, CA: TWFT Publishers, 1987.

Wysong, R. L. *The Creation — Evolution Controversy*. Midland, MI: Inquiry Press, 1976.